POSITIVE PARENTING, TODDLER DISCIPLINE & POTTY TRAINING (4 IN 1)

POTTY TRAIN YOUR TODDLER IN 7 DAYS OR LESS, EDUCATE WITHOUT SHOUTING & POSITIVE PARENTING STRATEGIES FOR HAPPY & HEALTHY CHILDREN

FAYE PALMER

© Copyright 2021 - All rights reserved.

The contents of this book may not be reproduced, duplicated or transmitted without direct written permission from the author.

Under no circumstances will any legal responsibility or blame be held against the publisher for any reparation, damages, or monetary loss due to the information herein, either directly or indirectly.

Legal Notice:

This book is copyright protected. This is only for personal use. You cannot amend, distribute, sell, use, quote or paraphrase any part or the content within this book without the consent of the author.

Disclaimer Notice:

Please note the information contained within this document is for educational and entertainment purposes only. Every attempt has been made to provide accurate, up to date and reliable complete information. No warranties of any kind are expressed or implied. Readers acknowledge that the author is not engaging in the rendering of legal, financial, medical or professional advice. The content of this book has been derived from various sources. Please consult a licensed professional before attempting any techniques outlined in this book.

By reading this document, the reader agrees that under no circumstances is the author responsible for any losses, direct or indirect, which are incurred as a result of the use of information contained within this document, including, but not limited to, —errors, omissions, or inaccuracies.

CONTENTS

TODDLER POTTY TRAINING & DISCIPLINE (2 IN 1)

Introduction	3

Part I
WHAT YOU SHOULD KNOW ABOUT TODDLERS

1. Getting to Know More About Your Toddler	13
2. Talking and Explaining Things to Your Toddler	28

Part II
YOUR BLUEPRINT TO GUILT-FREE TODDLER DISCIPLINE

3. Going for Positive Parenting Can Lead You to the Guilt-Free Method of Disciplining	45
4. Challenges of Positive Parenting that You'll Encounter	61
5. Practicing Patience	76
6. The Stress-Free Parenting Strategies to Raise the Happiest Toddler Around – Guilt Free!	90
7. Seeking Professional Help	104

Part III
LET'S TALK ABOUT POTTY TRAINING

8. When is the Best Time to Start Potty Training?	121
9. Deciphering the Facts, and Clearing Up the Misconceptions of Potty Training	131
10. Are You Mentally Prepared?	141
11. Getting the Equipment Ready	153

12. The 7 Step Plan for Potty Training Your Child in Just a Few Days	163
13. What to Do at Nighttime When Toilet Time Arises...	174
14. Getting Help from Daycares and Caregivers	185
15. Raising the Happiest Child Around	198
Conclusion	211

POSITIVE PARENTING & EDUCATING WITHOUT SHOUTING (2 IN 1)

Introduction	219

PART I

1. Starting the Journey in Harmony	227
2. Taking Stock of Your Parenting Style Before You Start	240
3. Brain Research and Child Development	253
4. Importance of The First Few Years	263
5. Emotional Intelligence	280
6. Role Models to Look Up To	291
7. Calm Responses in All Situations	300

PART II

8. Blocking Old Habits and Preventing Outbursts	315
9. Deep Connection, Unconditional Love	324
10. Building Trust and Emotional Bonds	332
11. Screen Time and Its Effects on Child Development	342
12. Child Development Opportunities from Positive Discipline	353
13. Speaking and Listening Skills	365
14. How to Go from Battlefield to Peaceful Place	377
Conclusion	391

TODDLER POTTY TRAINING & DISCIPLINE (2 IN 1)

THE 7 DAY DIRTY DIAPER FREEDOM GUIDE. THE STRESS FREE PARENTING STRATEGIES TO RAISE THE HAPPIEST TODDLER AROUND - GUILT FREE!

INTRODUCTION

Are you ready to take a deep dive into parenting? It does not have to be a sink or swim approach. Many parents feel at a loss for realistic parenting ideas. Others may think they have all the answers, but fall short when their offspring do not seem to fit the profile handed down from their parents and friends. Parenting can be exhausting, challenging and rewarding, all rolled into one adventure. A real life adventure.

This book, with its deep dive approach, will unpack many genuine ideas and guidelines to happy, healthy parenting. What qualifications do you think you need to be a parent? Teaching, nursing, a touch of psychology and some sports coaching will all find their way into your list of parenting skills. There is no 'one size fits all' to being a parent. A book like this will open your eyes to different perspectives offered in the parenting niche.

There is no wide road, with a supersonic car, to get to your destination. It really doesn't matter what walk of life you come from or your educational background. Your qualifications, your age, and your experience in life will contribute to your parenting skills. However, navigating the unexpected twists and turns on this parenting journey may bring you some surprises. In my experience, parenting is challenging. There is no simple formula to follow. The greatest difficulty comes with trying to manage individual characters and personalities. Children have different strengths and weaknesses. They grow and develop at different rates. Children are not built to fit a common mold. It really comes down to experience and being open to trying new ideas. Every parent will find themselves having to 'circle back' on their journey and try other tactics. This book is full of practical and thoroughly researched ideas on parenting for just that kind of situation. If at first you don't succeed then you can try again.

'Start with the end in mind,' is one of the principles of parenting I read in Stephen Covey's book on the 7 Habits of Effective Families. It is easy, as a parent, to feel you're floundering in a sea of diapers and discipline problems. Goal setting is a very important part of raising a family. I wish I had that simple principle in mind when I first started parenting. Books of all kinds are a great asset, but knowing what your goals are, is a very helpful principle to put in place. Through reading different publications, articles and parenting websites I have been struck by how much valuable information is available. The novice parent wants to devour every scrap of information. There are never enough hours in the day when you start out with your new baby. Finding a book that offers practical ideas, and is well researched, really helps sharpen parenting skills.

Kahlil Gibran, in the Prophet, uses a powerful analogy to bows and arrows to show a parent's role in preparing their children for life. He says:

"You are the bows from which your children, as living arrows, are sent forth."

How does this analogy resonate with parenting?

- A bow needs to be flexible to create the ability for the arrow to fly forward towards the target. In the same way parenting styles need flexibility, and an added amount of strength to stand firm in the face of adversity. Parents will find in the pages of this book strengthening and encouraging messages. Positive guidelines to assist the bow.
- The string of the bow must be strong and stretch to give added power to the flight of the arrow. There are times in your parenting journey when that string will seem stretched to its utmost capacity. The string, representing your parenting principles, needs to be able to hold fast and keep strong to ensure that arrow travels towards its target.
- The aim must be accurate to enable the arrow to find its way, straight and true, on its flight path. This is where having parenting goals, and knowing what your aim is, will count the most. The arrow will fly in the direction you aim for and having that end in mind will always help you find the true path for your arrow to follow.
- The arrows, the offspring your children, need feathers to

guide the arrow through the air. The feathers or fletching are not just random decorations they are carefully chosen wing feathers needed for guiding the arrow on its flight path. Your parenting styles are those feathers you choose to attach to that arrow. They help to send the arrow flying through the air destined to make its mark and reach the target. Turkey feathers are reputed to be the best. In the production of the arrow the feathers are carefully chosen by sorting them into left- or right-wing groups. If the arrows are not sorted into their specific groups they bend in opposite curves. Feathers from the same wing side will fly in a straight and true flight path. If an arrow should spin or be disrupted in its path the feathers help to stabilize it in flight and make the arrow fly more accurately. Parents who choose sound complimentary parenting skills will feather their arrows and help them fly confidently.

- There is an archer, the overall guide of our universe. In the circle of life, the archer uses the bow, the parents to propel the arrows, the children in a purposeful manner. This is the nature versus nurture component of parenting. Nature gives our children gifts from the universal origins of nature, and parenting nurtures those gifts, to help children be the best they can be.

Parenting should not be a hit or miss affair. This book, filled with expert advice and tried and tested values, will help to stabilize the bows and guide the arrows in the right direction. There is an air of urgency for this parenting era of our lives. The urgency is brought about by the essence of time. Time is the thief that can come in the night and rob us of our joy. The most effective parenting window is in the early years of child development. If you get the recipe right during those impressionable years, the role of a parent becomes easier.

Benjamin Franklin said:

"Never leave 'till tomorrow what you can do today."

Those words ring true when you think about parenting. The months and years fly by as your child grows and reaches all sorts of developmental milestones. A parenting book, that challenges the way parents spend time with their children and the purpose behind their parenting strategy, is a valuable guidebook. This book aims to be the very book you turn to in times of need. No parent wants to be like the white rabbit in Alice in Wonderland. Totally at a loss for what to do and where to go he ends up muttering about having no time and disappears down a rabbit hole. Alice follows him into a world of chaos and confusion. The expression 'down a rabbit hole' refers to exactly that kind of experience. Parenting does not need to be a 'rabbit hole' journey. The window of opportunity for parenting is brief, so make the most of this valuable time.

This book aims to highlight some of the most important aspects of parenting and raising incredible children. The stakes are high and the road to success may take twists and turns, but with some practical guidelines parenting skills may become more manageable. This book calls parents to find out about positive parenting through guilt free discipline. Getting to know toddlers and how to communicate with them is a big step towards implementing your parenting boundaries and achieving your goals.

Find out how to turn obstacles into opportunities. Learn how to practice patience and understanding and keep clam when you feel you want to explode. There are times when professional help is your best option, and this book will give you guidance as to when and how you should seek professional help. There is a whole section devoted to potty training. The first real step your toddler takes to independence is learning how to use the potty. You get to ditch diapers forever and have a little being who can use the bathroom successfully.

Really, at the end of the day as they say, you want a happy motivated child. Raising a happy well-adjusted child is the most satisfying part of parenting. Getting there may seem daunting as the media exposes parents to so many dangers along the parenting journey. Being able to utilize the well-researched resources of a parenting book, filled with all the most relevant topics, is a great help. The importance of early childhood development can never be over emphasized.

Early childhood development takes place at a rapid rate in the first five years of a child's life. Physical, cognitive, social, and language skills are all aspects of child development parents can be actively involved in. Children need nurturing and support from their parents to reach their developmental milestones.

This ancient Chinese proverb gives wisdom to the underlying truth behind parenting.

> *'I hear and I forget,*
> *I see and I remember,*
> *I do and I understand.'*

Another literal translation from the ancient Chinese saying ends with 'knowing is not as good as acting, true learning continues until it is put into action.'

The parent who is prepared to get into the pages of this book and put the advice into action is the one who will gain the most. Parenting styles need to be flexible but some elements of parenting never change. Giving love, security and support in our modern world are key elements. Putting them into practice with the help of tried and trusted methods and guidance help parents lighten the load on their parenting journey. Take this opportunity to get into the pages of this book and enjoy the challenge of active parenting as you 'do and understand.'

I

WHAT YOU SHOULD KNOW ABOUT TODDLERS

1

GETTING TO KNOW MORE ABOUT YOUR TODDLER

"Knowledge is power. Information liberating. Education is the premise of progress, in every society, in every family."

Said Kofi Annan who was secretary general of the United Nations and co-winner of a Nobel Peace Prize.

What knowledge should you have to power you up and set you off to a good start in the early stages of parenting? Getting into the head of a toddler is a challenging thought. Knowing all about the first few years of your toddler's life may seem overwhelming. The toddler years are probably the most exhausting. It is hard to imagine that a tiny tot can actually derail a family, but it can happen. The first chapter of this book should help you, as parents, to get a deeper understanding of the little person you have brought into this world. Raising a toddler does not have to be an emotional rollercoaster ride.

Let's start by looking at what you bring to the party. Imagine you were planning to start a business venture. You may frown at the thought. What do business and parenting have in common? Well actually there are many aspects of running a business that could relate to raising your family. Think of yourself for the moment as the manager. You would have strategies in place and more importantly you would need to know about your product.

Richard Branson said:

> *"A big business starts small."*

He probably wasn't thinking about raising a family, but through the eyes of this chapter you can adapt some valuable business ideas and put them into practice through useful parenting skills. Getting to know your toddler, the small component of this venture, is going to be a great help. Getting to know yourself will be an advantage too. How do you fit into the parenting business model?

A good place to start is with a S.W.O.T analysis.

S - strengths
W - weaknesses
O - opportunities
T - threats.

Have a real look at your family structure and with other family members take some time to be objective and see how you measure up.

Strengths would be your knowledge about parenting. You may have had parenting experience already. Perhaps you have had training in the field of education or child development. Did you come from an awesome family? Do you have great role models to follow? Are you an avid reader of parenting books? Do you have the time to spend being a great parent and do you feel you have the means to provide well for your family? You have probably found many strengths in the parenting niche.

Weaknesses nobody likes to focus on their weak areas, but this is a good way to watch out for pitfalls and close the gaps you may think are weak areas. Are you a first-time parent and feeling less confident than you should with little experience? Perhaps your own childhood was rather shaky, and you fear making the same mistakes or overcompensating because you want to do better? Do you feel you don't have enough time to put into the business of raising a family? Weakness can become strength with the right tools and knowledge to help you.

Opportunities are abundant. Raising a family is filled with an incredible number of opportunities. Relationships to build with your children. Educational paths to follow and family activities and events to enjoy. You have the opportunity to build character, and develop and nurture little people as they grow into bigger people. Parenting gives you the chance to be a good role model and a confidant and support for your family. Knowledge of how to embrace these opportunities will strengthen your parenting skills.

Threats, the barriers that get in the way of your parenting progress will always be there, but they can be overcome. There may be some threats you identify before you start this journey. Perhaps you struggle to balance your time as a busy working parent. Maybe other family members are interfering or perhaps your social circumstances are challenging. Threats will always be out there.

Henry Ford said:

"Whether you think you can or think you can't – you are right."

One of the threats to realistic parenting could be lack of knowledge about the very important early years. The first few important years of a toddler's life are vital stages of development in so many developmental areas. Learning about those early years will shed light on ways to get off to a great start.

If you could literally get inside your toddler's mind you would be amazed at the miracle of nature that is right there in the head of a toddler. Did you know a baby is born with 86 billion neurons? These are the cells in the brain responsible for receiving sensory information from the outside world. During the early years of development, the brain is very sensitive and the things it experiences can have a lasting effect on the child's emotional well-being. The brain is developing rapidly from birth to the age of five. Quality experiences are what matter the most and help to shape the brain.

A baby is born with the ability to learn. Right from day one and during the course of the first year the brain is growing and doubles its size. This growth continues and by the age of three the baby's brain has reached 80% of its adult size. The baby's brain has all the neurons it needs to cope with this growth and by the age of five, 90% of this growth has taken place. It is positive, stable nurturing that enables these neurons to grow. Your baby needs to feel nurtured and safe.

I remember bringing my newborn home for the first time. An exciting and scary moment all at once. One of the things that I thought was going to be difficult was handling the baby's' fontanel or soft spot. Imagine how much more nervous I felt when I found out there were several of them. Fontanels are soft spots on the baby's skull. I think most people are aware of the one on the top of the baby's head. Why are there soft spots just where the brain is developing? Well, there is a good logical reason. The soft spot, where the bones have not closed, gives the skull flexibility during the time the baby has to pass through the birth canal. The small openings in the skull allow the brain to grow while there is still some space and room for growth. The soft spot is actually quite resilient. It has a tough membrane over it. This spot is a good indicator of illness or dehydration. Most importantly it is allowing the brain to grow and develop at the rapid rate mentioned earlier. Remember your doctor will always tell you if there were any problems at birth and if you're concerned you can seek professional help.

Millions of connections are made every second as different areas of the brain prepare for the ability to move, understand language, and experience emotions. As the brain develops it builds on itself and the connections link with each other. During these early years the brain begins to develop higher order abilities like motivation, and problem solving. Loving healthy relationships with their parents is an essential ingredient to nurture communication and self-regulation. These abilities are encouraged through positive interaction with their senses.

Developing awareness to the five senses stimulates this development. Cooing, smiling, laughing and crying are all ways your little one is starting out on the road to communication with you and others.

How does this work? Dale Carnegie, motivational speaker and writer had this to say about positive interactions.

> *"Act enthusiastic and you will be enthusiastic."*

No matter how crazy it may seem you can coo, sing, laugh and play with your child often and the enthusiasm will be rewarded with something you cannot see. Now you know it is happening. The neurons in your child's brain are responding positively. Loving relationships with caring parents and child carers are an essential part of healthy development. The early years just fly by and knowing how much development takes place in just the first three months will have you astounded. Motor skills seem to get off to a slow start with head movements followed by the body, arms, and legs, but by eight weeks your baby has noticed their hands. The senses have already been busy, and your baby could smell and taste while still in the womb. Babies are startled by noise and your baby could hear in utero. Eyesight is the least developed of the senses, but babies do enjoy bright colors and moving objects. The sense of touch is highly developed, and babies respond to touch and movement. The brain associates touch with cognitive and social development. All these sensory skills are being developed in the little head where your baby's brain is growing and learning how to respond to the world.

The knowledge of how important the first years are is empowering for parents. You have the early development of your child in your hands. There are early milestones in every infant's life to celebrate and take credit for. Celebrating these milestones will motivate you as parents. Baby journals and baby books marking the journey as you go along the parenting road are encouraging. I remember how enthusiastic I was for the first baby and every little growth event. Filling in those baby milestones seemed very important. There were first times for everything. There was always a background to these accomplishments. Reaching a milestone does not always come easy so it is good to celebrate these occasions.

Mahatma Gandhi said:

"Every worthwhile accomplishment big or little, has its drudgery and triumph: a beginning, a struggle, and a victory."

That statement is so true of raising a child. The toddler years are probably the ones with the greatest struggle. It is at this point you may discover your child has characteristics you find hard to understand. You may think you have a racing demon on your hands. Toddlers are very busy people. Toddlers arrive in our lives somewhere between twelve to eighteen months. They are unsteady on their feet at first, but soon gain confidence. This is the age of discovery. It is an age of great cognitive and social development.

During this phase toddlers move around a lot more. They are more aware of themselves and what is going on around them. They want to explore everything. You need eyes in the back of your head to watch these little people. Toddlers begin to be independent and show defiance in some situations. Keeping up with a toddler can be exhausting. Trying to understand some of their behavior can be confusing. Without some understanding of why they behave like they do, a battle of wills could be the outcome.

Here are some tried and trusted tips to help towards dealing with unwanted behavior:

Tip #1 - Ignore the behavior you dislike

Toddlers are at what is known as the 'pre-operational' phase. Your toddler is thinking, but not using logic to transform or separate ideas. Your toddler is learning about the world, but not able to use the information they have learned. Starting to talk introduces this stage. This is a very egocentric stage of development. Toddlers focus on only one aspect of what is happening at one time. During the pre-operational stage toddlers learn by repeating behaviors. A big reaction for something they do is going to mean they want to repeat that behavior. It may be a naughty word or an action you disapprove of. Anti-social, bad manners or unkind actions are not the kind of behaviors you want to encourage.

Toddlers are involved in what is known as parallel play. They don't play with other children, but rather play alongside them in what appears to be play. At this stage of their social development, they do not really socialize with another individual their own age. You may wonder if this form of play is beneficial. It is a great steppingstone to language development, imaginative play and a pathway to understanding social interaction. Parallel play means your child is not functioning in an isolated world. They are involved in observing and getting ready for the next step in their social development.

Parallel play is a behavior you grow to like at this stage. It is positive and to be encouraged. Try not to interfere, but allow your toddler to go through this phase and watch your toddler grow and develop. Ignore the bad behavior unless it is going to harm or injure another child.

Tip #2 - Try not to use the no word too often

The no word seems to feature very soon in a toddler's vocabulary. This is probably because they hear it often. Think about how many times a day you say no. Toddlers soon learn to say the no word too. They begin to realize they have feelings and needs and wants too. Assertive behavior comes with the no word. Parents can try to lead by example and not say no to everything. Think of some alternatives and try to turn negatives into positives with the way you say things. Distractions and alternative behaviors work well. Instead of saying 'No jumping on the bed,' say let's rest on the bed and have a little nap. Act out the behavior and have a giggle together. Make everyday tasks fun.

Tip #3 - Don't exclude toddlers from everyday chores

It is much easier to get things done fast and the mundane chores are out of the way. Instead of saying don't do this or no to that try to include your toddler. Toddlers like to be involved and helping round the house has many benefits for growing children. It develops respect and a sense of being part of the family. Starting from an early age is a step in the right direction. Find little things your toddler can do and make a positive response to the action like praise for helping. My toddler went through a superhero phase and we became super helpful heroes. I made hero capes to wear while being a helpful hero and turning the chores into a game added value to the activity.

In the role of parent, you want to be the person Babe Ruth talks about. The basketball legend said,

> *"It's hard to beat a person who never gives up!"*

It is also hard to be the person who never gives up. The parent who is prepared to keep trying to understand how toddler behavior works. Why are toddlers defiant and is there a way to understand this behavior?

The answer is yes, there are ways to understand defiant behavior. Toddlers do not have enough vocabulary to express themselves clearly, but they do have very strong body language. They are very egocentric and at times even bossy. Take a look at some typical toddler communication through body language. What do these different stances really mean.

Cracking the code to toddler communication

<u>Pulling their shirt or dress up over their heads to hide away when they meet a new person.</u>

This action is a sign of anxiety. Your toddler is nervous to meet someone new and feels if they can't see the new person then that person can't see them. That makes the toddler feel safe.

What should you do?

Reassure your child and help them to warm up to the new person. Encouraging conversation and support through this time.

Your toddler won't make eye contact with you.

They look away or hold their heads down.

This action shows embarrassment. A sign of feeling ashamed about something they may have done. They know they may have done something to displease you.

What should you do?

Ask your toddler if they need to show you something. This may lead to the place where the accident happened. When you find out what it is, try not to overreact and rather discuss what they did and how it happened. You want your toddler to feel they can share things that worry them with you.

At bedtime your toddler insists on piling every single toy they have onto the bed!

Your toddler is beginning to use imaginary ideas. They may be afraid, but at the same time, they are pretending to be protected by toys.

What should you do?

Imagination is something you want to encourage. It is one of the higher order thinking skills. Try suggesting three toys will be enough and help your toddler to choose the three best toys for the job of protecting you.

Brattish behavior is very embarrassing.

Why do toddlers manifest such shocking behavior? Nine times out of ten it is to get your attention. Yes, negative attention is often better than no attention at all. Your child may be bored, tired or even hungry.

What should you do?

Address the three issues mentioned above if you feel that they may be the cause of the behavior. If you're on an outing always have a little bag of distracting toys or books. Play a different game with your toddler. If you feel this is genuine naughty willful behavior take some time out with your child and gently, but firmly tell your toddler breaking toys and being rough is not OK.

Clingy and overly possessive behavior.

Why do toddlers suddenly become like clinging vines? Hanging onto your legs as you try to walk or pulling on your cardigan. Just clinging onto you with such determination never to be separated. Your toddler could be telling you they need to spend more time with you. Have you been away or are they just starting out at play school? There could be a number of reasons why your toddler is trying to show you they need more of your time.

What should you do?

Think about the different issues or circumstances that could be demanding your time more than in the past. What has changed and how can you show your toddler that you can spend time with them and manage any changes too.

Weird antics like striping naked for a dip in the duck pond.

Putting weird objects like peas into their ears, drinking bath water and getting covered in mud. This is exploration at its best as long as it is not dangerous.

What should you do?

Have a good laugh and enjoy the moment. Capture the scene on your camera and share it with your child's grandparents. Get your toddler to join in the funny moment and laugh together. Parenting can have its moments of comic relief.

All this defiance and difficult behavior is part and parcel of growing up. It is the time in a toddler's development that they begin to realize they can have some control over their world. One of the ways to assert control is by defying you. Toddlers need to start doing things for themselves and gain confidence in themselves. Standing up to their primary caregiver is the start to this ability to gain independence. However, there have to be set limits and boundaries in place. Be prepared to show empathy and encourage children to talk about feelings. Offer choices, but make sure they are going in the right direction. A choice of pajamas for example still leads to going to bed. Decide on your end goal and work towards achieving that end result.

Keeping routines is very important for toddlers. Stick to times and the normal order of the things you do. Toddlers don't like change. The moment you try to do something in a hurry and out of their routine your toddler will become defiant and may well have a tantrum. If you have to do something out of routine make sure they are prepared. Add in something fun or if you're going on an outing take a toy or book along.

Helping your child to understand feelings is another way of helping them to grow through this phase. Help them learn about anger, sadness, happiness, and loneliness. Books are a wonderful tool to help toddlers to learn about feelings.

These books are available on Amazon:

The Color Monster by Anna Llenas - It is a pop-up book and very appropriate for this age.
In my Heart – A book of feelings by Jo Witek.
My Many Colored Days by Dr Seuss.
The Feelings Book by Todd Parr.

Books and stories are wonderful tools to help children understand their feelings.

In this first chapter it would be true to say understanding the toddler years and toddler milestones is a very valuable part of parenting. We started out recognizing knowledge is power. Knowing the truth behind milestones and behavior helps keep parenting in the early years in perspective.

Nelson Mandela, who knew about preparing for his long walk to freedom said:

"Remember to celebrate milestones as you prepare for the road ahead."

Take these ideas and your own personal goals as you get ahead in your parenting journey and reach milestones to celebrate along the way.

2

TALKING AND EXPLAINING THINGS TO YOUR TODDLER

"The world's a stage. And the men and women merely players. They have their exits and entrances; and one man in his time plays many parts."

— WILLIAM SHAKESPEARE

Learning to communicate with your infant and toddler will soon make you feel like an actor. It is time to put on your hat and cloak and set foot on the stage. A metaphorical stage, where you and your child will play different parts as you grow to know and understand each other. This new world of communication calls for some acting and amateur dramatics. Learning how to communicate with a toddler will require losing some inhibitions and learning how to give comical speeches, soliloquies, lectures, some solo singing, maybe a duet or two. Your world could easily become a stage as you learn different communication skills.

Communication begins from the day you bring your child into the world. The moment you're handed your little bundle of humanity you're ready to get to know each other. Exchanging glances, soft sounds of your voice and the way you touch your baby are all signs of communication. Your baby will make crying noises and soon you will get to know what they mean. Hunger, discomfort, needing attention are all the basic elements of communication. When your baby gives back the first sounds of cooing and gurgling you feel totally elated. It is instinctive to return the complement and coo and gurgle too. You have started your first little 'conversation' with your baby.

Jim Henderson, creator of the Muppets and the TV show Sesame street had this to say:

> "The most sophisticated people I have ever known had just one thing in common: they were all in touch with their inner child."

This is exactly where you want to be as you begin to communicate with your child. Lose inhibitions and imitate baby's vocalizations. The high-pitched squeaky voice many people use to talk baby talk sounds more nurturing. The baby relates this sound to being nurtured. Learning how to talk to a baby and a toddler is all about getting in touch with your inner child.

How does baby's speech develop from birth to a year? Timelines are interesting to look at, but parents must remember each child is an individual and times may differ.

One to three months:

Your infant loves to hear your voice. Babies may coo and gurgle and you may hear a vowel sound like ooh. Smiling in response to your voice is a reward at this phase. Did you know it is not too early to start reading stories at this age? The sound of your voice reading helps to stimulate the brain. Singing simple songs to soothe the baby are a good idea. Try a gentle lullaby.

Four to seven months:

Your baby is more aware of sounds and at this age babies watch their parent's reactions. They gurgle and make louder noises. You can start looking at picture books like board books or cloth books. Choose ones with simple pictures and say the word for the picture.

Eight to twelve months:

The noises your baby makes begin to sound clearer. Ma-ma and da-da may be heard with a ga-ga in between. Interaction with you is such fun. You can wave, clap hands, blow kisses and make other simple gestures. These interactions are all part of communication.

As you enter the next year of development, it is time to really get in touch with the child in you. Do you remember what it was like to be a child? What are some of the things you remember doing that encouraged language development? All those funny nonsense nursery rhymes will jog your memory and now you can play them with your child.

There are well loved rhymes like pat-a-cake and the Little Pig who went to the Market. Guaranteed to bring laughter and squeals of delight. There are many more infant rhymes you can learn to say and perform the actions. Imitation is a great way to learn. Try some simple dance moves with hand clapping. Toddlers love to dance and join in the chorus line.

Another way of encouraging language is to talk about what you're doing as you go about different activities. Say out loud what you're doing to bath or dress your toddler. Talk about the food they eat. Point out things they see in the garden or along the road. Toddlers can start to learn their colors and count a few numbers. Most of their learning will be imitation, but slowly the meaning and the memory will grow, and a wider vocabulary will develop.

Learning the words and associating them with objects is the first building block to learning a language. Picture books are invaluable. Soon your toddler will be able to identify the pictures and then you can add in animal noises or animal homes to increase vocabulary and start word association. Children love pop-up books and sound books too. They never get tired of hearing an old favorite over and over again.

In the same way that actors learn their craft, parents can learn how to be a good speaker and just as importantly they can learn how to listen.

Nicole Kidman, during an interview about acting, said an actor must be willing and devoted and be able to adapt. She recognized the need to adapt, because in acting the characters are always different. On your stage of developing communication skills be ready to learn how to pay attention and how to encourage the audience, your toddler.

One of the most important adaptations you will need to make is finding the right listening skills to cope with a toddler. A child who is emerging as a little person, starting out in the realm of communication, needs to feel you're listening to them. Active listening is one of the most important parts of being a good listener. This means learning how to physically take part in listening. Engage with the speaker and let them know you're really listening to them. They have your attention. In this modern age of technology, it is so easy to be distracted. Your mobile phone is probably the most distracting piece of technology you have. The temptations to listen or look at what is happening, right there in your hand, on your mobile phone is a huge distraction from being an active listener.

What is an active listener? Here are some points to consider.

- The first step to being an active listener is to put yourself in a listening mode.
- You need to engage with the person who is speaking.
- Show them you're listening by making eye contact.
- Nod and make little comments along the way.
- Ask questions about the topic being spoken about.
- Don't criticize, interrupt, or judge the person you're listening to no matter how small they are.
- Check your self along the way, if you feel bored, distracted, or feel you're wasting your time, then you're not really

listening.

Your actions, facial expressions, and body language are all part of being an active listener. Being a good listener builds self-esteem and confidence in the child you're listening to.

However, there is a limit you may be saying to yourself. How do you let children talk and be a good listener, but at the same time take into account that sometimes there needs to be a stop button? Life is actually a balancing act in so many ways! Letting your child have time to hold center stage, and time to acknowledge other people need to have a turn, is an important life skill.

As children grow more confident in their language skills and develop more vocabulary they may start to interrupt or dominate conversation. What do you do if you find your child is falling into this category of talking too much? You want to curb their conversation with some gentle reminders that others need a turn too. Here are some ideas.

1. Be patient, because after all you want to encourage language development. Have a secret sign you can share with your child to say it's mom's turn, or time to let someone else speak.
2. Show your child that taking turns even in speaking is important. Help your child to ask nicely if they may talk to you when you're with other people. Maybe they can say 'excuse me' or 'can I talk to you' and wait politely while you make sure they have a turn. It is important to respond to this

request or your child will get impatient and the idea won't work effectively.
3. Praise your child for their interesting ideas. If it is something they are clearly very interested in, take time to find other information or books on the topic. Children love dinosaurs for example and saying those complicated names is such fun. It is amazing how they will remember how to say Tyrannosaurus Rex, but forget to say thank you!

Now you feel ready for holding some form of conversation with your child. How do you initiate these talking times and how do you help your toddler to be able to join in with talking to you? The first step is to build up your child's vocabulary. Without the words to say something there will be no conversation. In the right nurturing environment children add to their vocabulary list at a rapid rate. In simple terms talking results in learning new words.

Here are some suggestions and ways to help build vocabulary and encourage conversations.

Read picture books together.

Point to the pictures and say the words. Make your reading experiences as interactive as possible. Children at this age love repetition. Get your child to copy you and parrot fashion say the names of the things pictured in the book. Sturdy board books are ideal for this activity. Use picture books for some play acting and mimicry. Make the noises of the animals, be the farmer planting the seed, drive the car and the bus in the pictures. One of my favorite books for these kinds of activities are the Richard Scary series. There is so much going on in each picture. Find a character you enjoy in the pictures and see what that character is up to each time you turn the page. Lowly Worm is a very endearing member of the Richard Scary stories and finding him in the picture is great fun for everyone.

Do things together and talk about the activity:

Make a point of talking about what you're doing and sharing an experience together. Baking is a wonderful way to share an activity together. There is the joy of mixing the ingredients and baking the biscuits. Licking the bowl and rolling out the dough encourages vocabulary development. Then when the biscuits are done have a tea party and invite other family members to join in.

Singing songs:

'Singalongs' are a wonderful way to be happy and learn through repetition. There are great action songs to help with learning vocabulary. Traditional nursery rhymes and new songs children learn at nursery school or from their older siblings are always cheerful ways to build vocabulary. Songs like Old McDonald can be creative too as your child learns the animals and the noises they make.

Learn how to use sensory words:

Children can start to understand their feelings through sensory words. Touch, taste and smell words can be encouraged through getting involved in the kitchen. Talking about how things feel can be developed with starting a sensory tray. Put different things on the tray to let your child feel soft, smooth, and rough textures. Make sure the objects on the tray cannot be swallowed. You want to avoid anything that could be choked on. A really easy way to check if an object is big enough to not be a choking hazard is to take a toilet roll and see if the object will pass through the cardboard roll. If the object does not fit through the roll then it is not a choking hazard. This simple method can apply to early toys as well.

The sense of hearing is developed through musical toys. The xylophone or maracas and drums all give a good range of sounds. Listening to pre-recorded sounds of animals or traffic noises will help develop the sense of hearing. You can go on a nature walk or visit a farm and put all five senses to the test.

Games develop language:

There are many suitable games to play to develop language skills. 'I Spy' is a good example. When children are young and don't know their letters, it is best to use colors to find the different objects. Tell your toddler you're looking for something red for example. Say – "I spy with my little eye something red". Obviously this game depends on your toddler knowing their colors.

Puzzle books and picture puzzles:

Books with picture puzzles like finding hidden objects are good vocabulary developers. At preschool children will learn about figure ground perception which involves looking for images among other images. This is an important part of learning how to discriminate letters later on. Start puzzles and discussions around pictures early on for vocabulary development and visual perception.

Puppets:

Puppets are wonderful little companions and teachers too. Have a basket of hand puppets to play with and use for interesting conversations. Your toddler may find it easier to act out or have imaginary conversations playing with a puppet. Puppets can say what they want and perhaps help with some frustrations your child may be experiencing. Parents can use puppets too as a spokesperson. Language and vocabulary are encouraged through acting out stories and plays with puppets. Puppets are a great rainy-day activity as they can entertain the family Instead of the TV. Bring live shows into your home and let your toddler participate.

Peek-a-boo puppets:

Playing games where puppets appear and disappear are one of the early interactive games children can play. Pop-up puppets that hide in fabric cones and pop up out of hiding can entertain a young child for hours. This act of knowing a toy can appear and disappear is an important child developmental milestone. The knowledge that something can appear and disappear is called object permanence. It is the beginning of understanding that if something hides away it is still an object and may come back into the game.

Puppet shows and storytelling:

Puppets have the potential to improve literacy through putting on little puppet plays or retelling stories. Many children feel more confident when they have a puppet at their fingertips. If you don't have any puppets a simple paper bag with a funny face on the front can make a puppet. An old sock transforms into a lively sock puppet and your child has the opportunity to create the puppet and then play with it as well.

Having conversations with your children can be very entertaining and enlightening too. Here's one that may make a bossy mom feel her parenting skills are rather pedantic.

> **Son:** Mom, why do the bad guys always try to win?
> **Mom:** Well, they want to be the boss and make all the rules.
> **Son:** Then they should try to be moms!

Little people can be very astute when it comes to running the house. However, there is one area of house and home that needs to be addressed and an area where good habits are important. That is personal hygiene. Children will not automatically learn how to be responsible for their cleanliness. Parents need to teach this to their children and to lead by example.

Personal hygiene starts with learning to wash hands. Teach your little one to wash hands at special times. Make sure the bathroom is user friendly for a tiny tot. A stool to stand on in front of the wash basin. A cloth and soap to use and a hand towel to dry hands with. At first your toddler will need help with this activity and reminders too. A handy chart with pictures showing when to wash hands will help capture the message for a tiny tot who is not able to read yet. Show your toddler how to fill the basin with just enough water and use the soap to lather their hands, rinse, dry, and to leave the basin clean for the next person.

Personal hygiene areas include:

- Hand washing
- Bathing
- Oral hygiene
- Hair care
- Toilet routine
- Sneezing and coughing risks – cover your mouth
- Cleaning finger and toenails

Bathing:

Bathing will initially be an activity you're both involved in. Bath time can be lots of fun with bath toys and bubbles and a great way to end the day. Teach your child how to wash all the important parts of their body and help with any areas you feel they are not able to wash at first. A non-slip mat in the bath is a great help with keeping your toddler from slipping in the bath water. Getting dry after the bath is another aspect of learning how to complete the bath routine. Use this as language building time too as you speak about what you're doing at each part of the routine.

Dental hygiene:

You can start your toddler early with getting used to having a toothbrush in their mouth and being shown how to brush. Making dental hygiene a part of the early morning and evening routine ensures this will be kept up. Include tongue brushing and give the roof of the mouth a scrub too. The importance of tooth brushing will need to be emphasized when the second teeth arrive. Children can learn to floss when they can manage this more difficult activity. An early introduction to the family dentist just to visit and experience the dental chair will help prepare your child for dental checkups.

Coughing and sneezing:

Covering your mouth and nose while coughing or sneezing is a very good habit to teach your child. Sneezes and coughs spread diseases readily into the air. At the same time, you can teach your child how germs are spread through the eyes, nose, and mouth. Putting dirty hands into these places spreads germs. Nose picking is a toddler habit that spreads germs into the nasal passages.

Hair care:

Washing and brushing hair usually acts as part of the bath routine. Toddlers do not really enjoy having their hair washed. Try to soften the experience with baby shampoo that does not sting eyes. If your toddler will wear one, there are shower visors that will prevent the water from running into their eyes. An attachment to the taps will make the hair washing activity less traumatic.

The toilet routine:

Toilet routines are part of the whole learning experience attached to potty training. Details of how to train your toddler to use the potty and subsequently the toilet is dealt with in more detail later in this book. The essential parts of toilet training for the hygienic routine will be washing hands and keeping clean while using the toilet or potty. Training and routines are different for boys and girls, but the essence of cleanliness is the important message to share as the training takes place.

Nail care:

Nails need cutting and cleaning because they are the ideal places for dirt and germs to live and grow. Toddlers will need help with clipping their nails. They can be shown how to use a nail brush and scrub up those dirty nails while they are bathing.

Introducing children to good hygiene habits is an important life skill and although it is a serious matter for health reasons bathing and washing can be fun times too with catchy tunes and bath toys to encourage joyful bath experiences.

Bath time can double as an opportunity to overcome any fear of water and teach children how to blow bubbles in the water by blowing out and not breathing in. This is a good exercise in preparation for swimming.

Use bath time as a bonding time and an opportunity to talk about the day and highlights your child may remember. There will be a chance for some loving cuddles at the end of bath time as you wrap your toddler in a fluffy towel.

Now you're ready for the final act of the day, a curtain call, and bedtime.

II

YOUR BLUEPRINT TO GUILT-FREE TODDLER DISCIPLINE

3

GOING FOR POSITIVE PARENTING CAN LEAD YOU TO THE GUILT-FREE METHOD OF DISCIPLINING

Positive parenting and feeling guilt free is something every parent would want to cultivate. Growing children who bring joy to parents and become upright citizens of society is a goal worth striving for. Gardening and feeling close to nature have some interesting parallels to parenting.

Here's a little rhyme to make you think about keeping close to nature and developing your parenting philosophies. It's advice to a gardener.

> *Grow peas of mind,*
> *Squash selfishness!*
> *Turnip to help your neighbor*
> *And make thyme for loved ones.*

Positive parenting and guilt free discipline definitely go hand in hand towards helping parents and children grow in the right direction.

What memories do you have of discipline while growing up? What does discipline mean to you?

I had a serious think about the discipline I experienced as a child and then the modified version of that discipline I used in my parenting. I guess we are all results of our childhood experiences, but with research and greater understanding of how children develop today parenting styles have changed.

Punishment erred on the corporal side as we grew up. A spanking, as opposed to a beating, seemed acceptable. Spare the rod and spoil the child was a favorite parent expression. Parents who did not hand out corporal punishment were seen to be too soft on their children, too progressive. Children were expected to be seen and not heard or put in the 'naughty corner' with their noses pressed to the wall. Almost humiliated for what they had done. Old fashioned parenting did not encourage reasoning with children. It did not take into account that children went through different stages in their development. Parents did not realize the effect corporal punishment had on their children, but no alternatives were really offered. Discipline styles were handed down from one generation to the next.

One thing gardening and children have in common is tending to a garden, and raising children, requires learning and adaptability.

> *"Gardening is learning, learning, learning. That's the fun of them. You are always learning."*

said actress Helen Mirren.

Parenting falls under the same umbrella. Parents are always learning about their children and parenting. Like gardening, seasons change, weeds are removed and pruning needs to be done. Nurturing is important and watering too. Gardening is an ongoing occupation. Parenting keeps you busy! However, with knowledge and understanding there are many joyful moments as your offspring blossom and grow to become healthy adults.

What kind of seeds do you want to sow? Seeds of criticism, negativity, anger, and frustration? That is what negative parenting can do. In today's studies of child development and how children respond to various forms of discipline, psychologists have found harsh physical discipline results in children who are angry and defiant as they grow older. Children were made to blindly fall in line with harsh parenting. Fortunately, parents today do not have to raise their children with harsh, dictatorial, parenting styles.

Positive parenting is one of the most enlightening forms of parenting and is offered to parents through the eyes of psychologists and professionals who have studied the subject and willingly share their knowledge. Through positive parenting you can enjoy one of the most fulfilling and rewarding parts of the cycle of life. Positive parenting is the way to approach raising your child in today's world filled with more obstacles than your parents or their parents before them.

"Children, marriages, and gardens reflect the kind of care they get."

A quote from H. Jackson Brown Jr, an American author, who wrote an inspirational best seller called Life's Little Instruction Book.

He also wrote, "Live so that when your children think of fairness, caring, and integrity they think of you." This could be the essence of positive parenting. It is about a legacy you pass onto your children through the way you raise them. Positively you help them grow up learning about respect, making friends, wise choices, and accepting there are consequences to their actions. Resilience and honesty and a good work ethic are other byproducts of positive parenting.

What exactly is Positive Parenting you may ask. Here are a few basics to the concept before taking a more in depth look at parenting in a positive way.

- Positive parenting is teaching, guiding, caring, leading, and nurturing.
- It is providing for children's needs with good communication.
- Positive parenting is non-violent and about positive relationships.
- Positive parents provide affection and emotional security.
- It rewards achievements and supports children's best interests.
- Positive parenting sets boundaries supporting mutual respect.
- It strives to teach discipline in a way that builds self-esteem and is consistent.
- Happiness is the main focus of positive parenting and all caregivers, family members and extended family and friends are involved.

- Positive parenting is thoughtful, kind and loving, but not permissive.

Research from organizations involved in parenting and psychologists report there is evidence of positive outcomes relating to emotional health and social skills through positive parenting. Academic success, building confident children, intellectual, and social growth are all enhanced through positive parenting.

Punishment would always seem like the negative part of parenting. The thorn in the side. Who will be the big bad wolf and be the disciplinarian?

> "We can complain because rose bushes have thorns or rejoice because thorn bushes have roses."

said Abraham Lincoln.

Looking at parenting may make you feel you're dealing with thorny situations and your discipline gets in the way of a relationship with your child because you're always punishing. However, with positive parenting and a paradigm shift of looking at how punishment works in positive parenting you may be able to look at that thorny bush, your somewhat prickly child, as an object of beauty and something to be enjoyed in your proverbial garden of life.

The positive parenting approach to discipline means children's individual needs are taken into account. Children are treated with empathy and respect. Positive parenting and child development go hand in hand. The principles are put into practice not just for the duration of childhood but as a framework for the child's life.

Positive parenting skills work towards understanding a child's point of view, but at the same time share empathy with the demands on parents. Setting appropriate boundaries is an important aspect of this style of parenting. Boundaries are the guidelines for positive discipline. There is a balance between parents needs and the needs of the child.

Here is a table showing what **discipline with positive parenting is** and **what it is not!**

Discipline with positive parenting is....	Discipline with positive parenting is not....
It is a parenting philosophy with a strategic method encouraging the idea of building relationships with your children.	It is not an unstructured vague idea of just being nice to your child.
Positive parenting sets boundaries allowing parents to remain calm and patient.	Positive parenting is not slack and unplanned with no recognition for parents It does not create frustrated parents.
It aims to build real connections between parents and children with the goal of gaining the children's cooperation.	Discipline with positive parenting is not responsible for disconnecting you from your child through harsh or inappropriate punishment
Discipline with positive parenting is firm, but delivered with understanding and in a loving tone. It does not shame or criticize children.	Discipline with positive parenting is not irrational or negative. It is not physical or critical.
Positive parenting uses a concept of time-in not time out. Time in is about building and maintaining a relationship with your child.	There is no concept of time-out as a punishment. Time out says you as a parent are not able to handle the situation. Time out is a very negative approach to discipline.
Positive parenting builds self-esteem and respect.	Positive parenting style of discipline does not make children feel unworthy and negative about themselves.
Positive parenting discipline model builds children up and fosters self-confidence, strength of character, and valuable life skills.	Positive discipline does not alienate parents and children. It does not take away opportunities for positive character-building relationships.

One of the most important factors surrounding positive parenting is being constructive and setting goals. It is known for building up character and strength.

Rudyard Kipling, the well-known author of the Jungle Book, said:

"Gardens are not made by singing – Oh how beautiful and sitting in the shade!"

In the same way a parent who sits in front of the crib and gazes at their infant, expressing how beautiful the child is, without some serious parenting plan is not about to 'grow' a positive, well behaved, responsible child. Positive parenting is about being focused on discipline and raising a child who respects others, not through fear, but through knowing and following the guidelines set out by their parents.

Here are nine suggestions to follow offering guidelines to implement positive parenting and develop positive discipline.

1. Setting boundaries:

Boundaries are very important because they set the parameters you will work within. Knowing there is a boundary protects parents and nurtures children. Boundaries will need to be adjusted as children reach different stages in their development, but by having some simple boundaries from the beginning you're already on the road to positive parenting success. Boundaries will make the need to discipline easier and more logical.

2. Have consequences for children:

Children need to know that actions result in consequences. If they disobey or refuse to listen to sensible instructions, there will be consequences. It may be something simple like not wearing a cardigan in cold weather means you will get cold outside and may not be able to play with your friends. Facing up to consequences ties in closely with boundaries.

3. Avoid hurtful words that make children feel ashamed:

Children are sensitive to what you say about them. Cutting, unkind words with sarcasm may be very hurtful and damage self-esteem. Think carefully about what you say and how you say it.

4. Encourage connections through working and playing together:

Building a trusting connection between you and your child is a very positive part of parenting. You want your child to trust you and respect your decision making. Building positive connections will take time and effort. It will be worth the effort as your child will want to seek your advice later on in their journey towards adulthood.

5. Remember to be consistent about enforcing the principles you value as important:

You must be consistent in your approach to keeping the rules or boundaries you have set. Speak in a loving, but firm tone of voice. Don't let your child take control of the situation. you're the parent.

6. Consolidate good behavior with positive comments:

Noticing and remarking on the good things your child does is an important part of positive parenting. When you see something they have done that is a good form of behavior then say something to show you have noticed. This builds self-esteem and highlights the positive behavior you want to see.

7. Show respect:

Get down to your child's level as they go through various stages of maturity and acknowledge them by showing you have respect for their efforts. Show your child how you respect other people too. If you're wanting to see kindness in your child, you need to be kind to others and model this sort of behavior.

8. Work on showing empathy:

Try and understand the reasons behind different types of behavior. If you understand where the action is coming from then you will be able to empathize with your child at that time. Empathy means wearing the shoes of the other person.

9. Opt for time-in not time-out:

The goal of positive discipline is not to alienate you from your child and push them away. Time-out pushes children away because it separates the child from their parent. It does not help the child deal with the negative behavior. Time-in on the other hand brings parent and child together. It recognizes there was some undesirable behavior, but together the parent and child can try to resolve the situation. Time-in is not all about smiling and laughing, it is a serious time while you look at boundaries crossed, or safety rules broken.

Once you begin investigating positive parenting you will start noticing some of the benefits of this style of parenting. Parents say they experience fewer behavior problems. One of the most encouraging outcomes is the relationship that develops between parent and child. It is a closer relationship and an understanding between both parties. It creates an ongoing connection within families.

Positive discipline builds better self-esteem and more positive mental health. Children raised in the positive parenting mold have better social skills and are more well-adjusted. Emotional support is a key component of well-adjusted children who feel their needs are being met.

Children learn from the example their parents set. Yelling at children, calling them names, and dishing out physical punishment does not build healthy parent/child relationships. Children who misbehave consistently frustrate their parents. Taking the 'mis' out of misbehave is something parents would like to strive for.

Misbehavior is, behavior gone wrong. The action is incorrect, improper, or inappropriate. Misbehavior is an action that is not acceptable to other people. It can be thought of as misconduct, mischief and misdemeanor. All these words have negative connotations.

What can parents do to take the 'mis' out of 'mis' behavior? Here are some practical options to turn around a behavior you consider inappropriate.

- Take a moment to consider the behavior and use the opportunity to teach your child about the correct behavior. In other words, turn the incident into a learning experience. Acknowledge the behavior you did not enjoy and talk about how your child should behave to gain approval and be well behaved.
- Spend time finding ways to encourage problem solving. Don't always find the answers for everything. If a difficulty comes along help your child to find a positive solution. This may help overcome some frustrating behavior that could lead to misbehavior. Instead of getting mad because something won't work, problem solving together will help your child think for themselves, or ask for help.
- Always be ready to acknowledge feelings. If your child is battling with anger, disappointment, pain, or lack of self-control take time to recognize the feelings they have and understand the underlying problem.
- Take your child away from the situation causing the misbehavior. If you're in a situation that is adding to the misbehavior, then take your child out of this environment into a calmer space. It may be appropriate to actually go home sooner if you're out and want to avoid a conflict in public. Show you understand the situation or the stage of development they are in. Take time to acknowledge that your child is growing up and still learning many different things. you're offering support and guidance, not criticism and punishment.

Misbehavior, especially in a public place, is very embarrassing for parents. There are reasons why children take advantage of misbehaving. Did you know that one of the reasons children do misbehave in public is because it works? It is a learned behavior and young children are sharp enough to recognize this behavior effectively gets them what they want. Whining and throwing temper tantrums are a top favorite of misbehavior that leads to getting their own way. you're making a rod for your own back if you give into this form of misbehavior. Set the boundaries before you go shopping for example and make sure your child will not be demanding anything and everything they see. Here is an opportunity when they are old enough to teach your child about pocket money and spending what they have available at the time.

Misbehavior may be the result of power struggles. Your toddler wants to be in control. Argumentative and difficult behavior result when your child does not want to do as they are told. Take the mis out of this power-seeking behavior by giving your child two choices. That simply defuses the situation and makes your child decide on a preferred behavior. They are not opposing you because you have given them a choice, but they are still fulfilling the need to complete a task you have given. Perhaps you have asked them to tidy up their toys. Give them a choice to tidy up there and then or before their favorite TV program. The task still gets done, and you have avoided the misbehavior.

Take the mis out of misbehavior by being in tune with your toddler's needs. Most very young children still want to have primary needs fulfilled. Food, sleep, and comfort are among the most basic. Your child may just be wanting some attention, but may not have the communication skills to tell you their basic needs. Take time to be aware of these basics and provide for them. This could take the mis out of the fractious child who is really just missing sleep, food, a clean diaper, or just a cuddle from a busy mom or dad.

You may misunderstand your child's feelings, and this could lead to misbehavior. Teaching children about feelings and emotions and how to express them will help in some emotionally charged situations. Books are the perfect tools for learning about emotions. There are delightful books about feelings with pictures and words to explain the emotion. Reading, or looking at picture books, is a terrific way to help your child understand feelings.

Misbehavior may be because your toddler is trying to flex their muscles and be more independent, but actually they do not have the skills yet to be an independent person. Toddlers get very frustrated because they are not able to perform some simple tasks. They are often heard to say, "Me do," as they try to do many things independently. This is where you, as chief commanding officer, have to decide if what your toddler wants to do and can do are appropriate. If your son wants to wear his superhero cape to school and his hero mask, and it is not dress-up day, is it going to affect his school career as he does go ahead with this show of independence? No, it is not, so let your child go to school dressed in his favorite superman outfit. Just put a change of clothes in then he can change at school if he wants to. This is a situation where some flexibility and acknowledgment of independence are really not an issue.

Now here's a thought. Could you, the parent, be causing your toddler to misbehave?

There is a possibility that you're the reason for the mis in misbehave. Consider these scenarios and put yourself in your child's shoes. Maybe these are parent traps you could avoid.

Too busy!

you're not spending enough time, quality time with your child. This does not mean hours and hours of time when you're distracted doing other things. Sitting on the floor with Lego but reading your emails on your phone is not quality time – you're distracted. Perhaps your toddler has asked you to look at something he/she has done, but you're still looking at your phone and text messages. Your toddler gets frustrated and attracts your attention by misbehaving.

What to do?

Dedicate some quality time to your toddler especially if you're a working parent. Make eye contact, listen carefully, add comments to interact, and make conversation. Then when you have seen the wow factor of the moment explain to your toddler that you have something else to do. You have spent quality time not quantity time.

Modeling bad behavior!

You yell at home and have your own style of tantrums. You use bad language and on bad days are very moody showing your misbehavior in front of your toddler. Children will copy your behavior.

What to do?

Avoid displays of misbehavior in front of your child. It is a case of practice what you preach when it comes to the behavior you want to reinforce.

Not meeting basic needs!

Young children have some basic simple needs. Not the ones needing toys or sweets, but the need for sleep, food, and comfort. At a young age they feel angry because these needs are not being met. Recognizing those needs and taking care of them will avoid temper tantrums from children who know they need something, but are not even sure what it is, or how to tell you.

What to do?

Have a routine that you stick to. In that routine you will factor in mealtimes, nap times, play times, and bath and bedtimes. Stick to the routine to avoid misbehavior.

You set your sights too high!

If you're expecting a ten-year old's behavior style in a one-year old's body, then your expectations are too high. Toddlers are just emerging from the infant stage and are not fully grown mentally or physically by any stretch of the imagination.

What to do?

Know the milestones your toddler should have reached and make sure you observe how capable they are at each stage of development.

This chapter was all about making you think on the lines of positive parenting and how this approach to discipline has benefits for the whole family. Like tending a garden, it requires some work and diligence.

Audrey Hepburn once said:

> *"To plant a garden is to believe in tomorrow."*

The same philosophy applies to positive parenting, because raising a family means you believe in the future – your future and theirs.

4

CHALLENGES OF POSITIVE PARENTING THAT YOU'LL ENCOUNTER

Everyone is familiar with the "Keep calm and carry on sayings". Did you know the slogan originated from a prewar poster to lift the spirits of the British people? 'Keep Calm and Carry On' was one of three posters issued at that time. 'Your courage. Your Cheerfulness' was the second one, and a third slogan was – 'Your resolution will bring us Victory'. It is the 'Keep Calm and Carry On…. followed by all manner of reasons for keeping calm, that has survived since before the Second World War.

Keep Calm and Carry on Parenting could well be a mantra for concerned parents. Keeping calm during a storm is one of the challenges of positive parenting. The idea of keeping calm whilst steering your parenting ship comes with highs and lows. This chapter is about facing challenges and managing some nerve-wracking situations with your child.

> *"I'm not afraid of storms. I'm learning how to sail my ship."*

said Louisa May Alcott. Well known author of Little Women.

There is no doubt that parents can expect storms. Raising children is going to have its stormy moments. There will be times when you feel quite lost at sea, but having a parenting blueprint to follow and to refer to will always help you navigate the rough times. This blueprint to Positive Parenting will help you enjoy the days of calm when things are going well and help you see the fruit of your labors.

Making a decision to follow the Positive Parenting approach to raising your family will need planning and commitment. Along with that commitment comes the need for a calm attitude to lessen the stress of just being a parent. This method of parenting is conscious parenting. It is about planning and goal setting. While you're ready to practice Positive Parenting remember there is a theory behind the practice and it is this theory that keeps you calm and positive.

In our analogy to sailing and practicing Positive Parenting this quote rings true of the theory behind a positive style of parenting:

> *"He who loves practice without theory is like a sailor who boards a ship without a rudder and compass and never knows where he may cast."*
>
> — LEONARDO DA VINCI

Here is a brief outline of the theory behind Positive Parenting. It is a theory based on learning through social and developmental psychology. Positive Parenting strives to reach its goals through mutual respect, firm but fair boundaries, and positive communication skills. Parents are encouraged to build a strong bond with their child and to take on a leadership role. Parenting is about guiding children in a positive way through their childhood. It is a proactive style of parenting with positive discipline. These are the principles that provide the rudder and compass needed to know the direction your parenting ship is sailing.

Staying calm in the middle of a storm is a vital part of handling Positive Parenting. The development of a calm spirit in yourself is a personal strength to carry you through the difficult times. Some of these suggestions may seem obvious, but in spite of being aspects of life one should take care of, it is surprising how many parents overlook the fact that they need to be in good shape to be a positive parent.

Tips to Positive Parenting include:

A healthy lifestyle.

Eat well, get a reasonable amount of sleep, and take some 'time-out' for yourself.

Take deep breaths.

When a difficult situation arises, take some deep breaths before reacting.

Try not to yell.

Shouting only raises your stress levels and your child's.

Be a guide, not a field Marshall.

Remember your role in Positive Parenting is to guide your child through empathy and support during the different stages they are experiencing.

Find support.

Remember you're not alone at this time. Draw on help from family and friends. Find support groups with like-minded people to interact with and share experiences.

Remember you're not alone!

> *"The sooner we learn to be jointly responsible the easier sailing will be."*

Wise words from Ella Maillart, a traveler and adventurer.

This sentiment applies to parenting too. It is a joint responsibility and part of your plan for Positive Parenting needs to include the support system. Everyone in your support team needs to be on board for the Positive Parenting principles you plan to implement. Your support team will help you stay calm and relieve some of the stress you may be feeling.

The support team you have to depend on begins with your parenting partner. Whatever your circumstances' and whoever your partner may be, the essential ingredient to your partnership is to be following the same rules. If you agree on Positive Parenting be sure both parties are familiar with what this means and how to go about following this course from the beginning. Set your goals and boundaries together to be working towards the same end result.

Add family and friends to your support group.

Dodinsky, known as an inspirational writer and creator of inspiring quotes knew the value of support and the need of help in difficult times.

He wrote this interesting quote about the 'sea of life.'

"We are the captains of our own ships sailing the sea of life, but in times of stormy weather you will discover true friends when they don't hesitate to be the lighthouse."

Who will be your lighthouse?

There really is no shame in getting help and reaching out to like-minded people. These are the supporters you need because they will be willing to share their experiences with you. Your support group will help you stay calm knowing you're on the right track. The obvious supporter is your spouse or partner raising your child. Family, especially grandparents offer a support system, while relatives come in a close second on this list. Friends, especially the ones raising children at the same time, are good sources of support. Caregivers and childcare centers willingly give parents their support. Care centers often offer parenting workshops. These are great events to attend and get input on challenging topics.

One on one support can be supplemented through online sources of information and guidelines. Medical help is always available for the emergency situations and support groups geared towards specific problem areas always offer a positive means of information and support. In this global village we live in you're never alone or without support.

It is vitally important to discuss your parenting model before reaching out to others to be absolutely sure on the basic principles you're following. Ideally this 'talking it out' conversation should take place before the baby arrives, but it is never too late to discuss what your parenting objectives are. One of the key core values of parenting is to be flexible and review your approach as your child grows and faces different challenges.

In tackling problems at sea, a sailor finds that:

> "The pessimist complains about the wind, the optimist expects it to change, the realist adjusts the sails."
>
> — WILLIAM ARTHUR WARD

You have to be the realist and discuss your tactics with your partner. Here are some of the issues you will want to talk about together before disagreements come between you. A vital part of

Positive Parenting is having common goals and common ground rules.

1. Discipline

What style of discipline will you want to adopt? Do you want to use your own parents as role models, or do you feel parenting styles have changed and you're ready and open to something like 'Positive Parenting?' Discipline is probably the most controversial parenting subject, but it is impossible to implement Positive Parenting without a discipline strategy that both parents agree on.

2. Creating house rules together

What will you tolerate round the house? Agree on specific times and activities. A routine is important. There will be times when you have to be flexible, but generally on a day-to-day basis have a routine. This will include bath time and bedtime. TV time or other electronic devices, privacy of parent's room and as children grow older, they want their privacy too. As children grow older you may want to include some chores in your parenting strategy.

3. Consequences

Decide on the consequences to be faced for different situations and be sure your child knows they will face these consequences. Consequences are a part of parenting you will need to review often. Positive Parenting does mean there is flexibility in your plan, but any changes need to be discussed and put in place with mutual agreement.

4. Always support one another

Sticking to your parenting plan is very important and supporting one another too. Added to that support for the consequences your child will face must be part of your mutual agreement. Consequences will need to be reviewed as children grow and develop physically and emotionally. This means that you don't disagree in front of the children. If there is an issue take some time away from the children to discuss the issue.

5. Don't be unbending

Positive parenting allows for mistakes and is flexible. Recognize if something is not working and change your point of view. Discuss the matter and change the strategy if necessary. Don't be afraid to give second chances and make allowances for different personalities and characters in your family.

Yelling, shouting, and screaming are all very negative ways of communicating. Yelling does not help a parent to be in control of the situation. It is something I learned as a parent and as a teacher. Yelling, unless you're a drill Sargent, will not keep you in control of the situation. Eventually yelling just becomes a jarring noise and children tend to switch off from the terrible noise. It has been found that yelling can be as harmful as physical abuse. That is a very scary fact. Children who are yelled at are more likely to develop problematic behavior. Actually, a loud voice yelling at you constantly does not make the message clearer.

Yelling brings out aggression in children while calm behavior reassures children and makes them feel loved and accepted even if they have done something wrong. Yelling, that is accompanied by insults and negative comments, can be considered emotional abuse. Yelling does not get the required results and children don't listen to someone who yells. The persistent act of yelling leads to increased levels of anxiety, stress, and depression in young children.

We can learn great lessons from proverbs and sayings from different countries.

There is an African proverb that says:

> *"Smooth seas do not make a great sailor."*

In parenting terms, it is the times we are tossed around by different issues as parents that makes us stronger. Parenting is all about weathering storms and riding the waves of a rollercoaster journey. These experiences can be very stressful. How can parents manage stress while still holding to the positive parenting style?

What are the main causes of stress for parents? Stress stems from the demands that are made on parents that they feel cannot be met. Demands on time, from outside influences and from family issues. The stress of holding down a high-powered job and the stress of schools as well as financial stress. Stress affects anyone who feels anxious and under pressure. The demands of raising a child from infancy through the growing phases of childhood affects parents in particular in these areas.

- Time.
- Finances.
- Increased responsibilities.
- Demands on different relationships.
- Health issues.
- Self Confidence.
- Personal space.

These seven areas are common stress areas. Parents young and older, in different socioeconomic backgrounds or different educational surroundings, all experience these stresses while starting out as parents. Even seasoned parents, finding their feet with the next child to arrive in their family, will experience stress.

Every parent is different, and every child is different, but some relief from stress can be found with these helpful tips:

Time management:

- Get up fifteen minutes earlier to allow for unexpected things that could go wrong.
- Schedule unpleasant tasks for early on in the day, avoid delaying them till later.
- Make time to listen to some music, read a book, or just browse through a magazine. Giving yourself some quality time will enable you to have more energy for later in the day.
- Keep stocks of home essentials like toilet paper and sticky plasters so you always have enough and don't waste time going out to buy these basics.

Financial stress relievers:

- Get advice on managing finances with a reliable friend or financial adviser.
- Take care of the pennies and the pounds look after themselves is a well-known phrase about being thrifty. Have a budget and try to monitor your spending.

Coping with extra responsibilities:

- Don't rely on your memory for things you have to do. Make a list for the next day with the things to do and any appointment times.
- When you feel overwhelmed take some deep breaths and think through what you have to do. Prioritize and get things done in a logical fashion.

Personal relationships:

- Don't be afraid to say no to an invitation you don't have time for. Protect your personal boundaries.
- Spend time with positive people who are not going to add their worries to yours.
- Try to have a 'date night' with your partner.

Worrying about health issues:

- Take care of your health. Have a healthy diet, get enough

sleep and do some exercise. Keep hydrated with enough water to drink.
- Make sure all inoculations are up to date and any vaccines that will protect you and your family have been taken care of.
- Take the whole family, including the dog, out for a brisk walk. Getting fresh air if you can is important for the whole family.

Managing self-confidence:

- Don't be a doom and gloom person if something goes wrong think of all the things that have gone right.
- Keep a journal of personal feelings and positive outcomes.
- Eliminate self-destructive, negative talk.

Allocating some personal space:

- Put your phone on silent sometimes and take some time out for yourself. Ask your partner to mind the baby for you during this time.
- Don't schedule back-to-back appointments. Manage your schedule realistically with some space between appointments.
- Don't be afraid to delegate some tasks to others to free yourself up and take the stress off your shoulders.

These are just a few ways to manage the stress around what seems to be the most common stress areas. Discuss your stress pressure points with someone you trust or seek some counseling if it will help your family life and keep you positive.

Stress can lead parents to make rash decisions and make parenting mistakes. Since we are human, we are going to make mistakes. The Positive Parenting model is not perfect. It is easy to make mistakes. Everyone makes errors of judgment in difficult circumstances. Facing up to them and correcting them is harder. The power behind Positive Parenting is through building relationships. Parents in good steady relationships are in a position to recognize mistakes, discuss them openly and make changes to rectify the mistake.

Typical mistakes are usually found in parenting styles. The parent who is too controlling and does not allow the child to become self-reliant and independent is making a mistake that leads to a clingy child afraid to do things without their parents. The parent who is a poor role model makes the mistake of demonstrating negative behavior. In this situation a parent should not be surprised if their behavior has led to their child's bad behavior.

Being inconsistent is a big mistake. Inconsistent parenting is frustrating for children. They need strong leadership to feel secure. You can recognize this parenting mistake by the way you make decisions. Do you make inconsistent decisions and change your child's boundaries? Parents may make the mistake of being too critical or making unfair comparisons between siblings. Recognizing this mistake means a change of attitude to your child and making amends for the unfair comparisons.

It is a mistake for parents not to recognize and empathize with children's feelings. This may happen when parents are busy and do not have sufficient time to spend with their children. It takes time to form the bond that allows for a sharing of feelings between parent and child. It is a mistake to be insensitive to your children's feelings. Getting in touch with your own sensitivity and being able to recognize your child's feelings is an important part of Positive Parenting.

Martin Luther King Jr said:

"If you can't fly then run, if you can't run then walk, if you can't walk then crawl, but whatever you do you have to keep moving forward."

This is so true of learning from our mistakes. Mistakes don't have to hold you back and prevent you from moving forward. Take these simple steps when making mistakes and keep moving forward.

- Notice and recognize your mistakes.
- Think about why you made that mistake. Does it go back to your past or to a previous parenting style?
- Discuss the mistake with your parenting partner.
- Learn a lesson from the mistake and the underlying reason for making it.
- Apologize for making this mistake and make an apology that suits the age of the child and the nature of the offense.
- Take positive action to change for the future. Mistakes do happen it is how you deal with them that is important.

- Take the right steps to move forward and keep moving in a positive direction.

Learn from your mistakes, keep calm and carry on with positive parenting. Know what you're aiming for. Remember to have goals for your family and parenting plans to set sail on your ship regardless of storms and tempestuous seas to reach your destination.

5

PRACTICING PATIENCE

Parenting epitomizes patience. The essence of being a parent is patience and it is a virtue beyond all virtues. Without patience parents will struggle to fulfill the many facets of raising a child. Patience comes with other virtues like kindness. It brings peace and joy. Parenting and patience must go hand in hand.

Khalil Gibran's collection of philosophies describes parenting with love in a thought proving manner. And with love goes patience.

"You may give them your love, but not your thoughts. For they have their own thoughts. You may house their bodies but not their souls for their souls dwell in the house of tomorrow, which you cannot visit, not even in your dreams. You may strive to be like them, but seek not to make them like you. For life goes not backward, nor tarries with yesterday."

Although love conquers many things, love cannot function without patience. This quality, patience, is described as many things. It is known for being the ability to endure different struggles as we strive to reach a goal. In parenting terms, it may be something as simple as table manners or as challenging as potty training. Patience helps parents to recognize that success will come with patient endurance. Patience helps you to stay calm while trying to teach or train somebody in different skills. Patience allows parents to love unconditionally during tough times.

Parents will find they have limitations to their patience levels. This level of limitations will be different for every family. It is a part of Positive Parenting and parents need to recognize this within their own family dynamics. Your children will have their own thoughts and will want to do things differently as the Prophet reminds us. Our children are the future and parenting styles change to support the future goals of this new generation. Parents patience, and recognizing their limitations, is an important part of reaching their goals.

There are several common parenting limitations. Most of them are based on surrounding circumstances and some on the parent's temperament and personality. When parents recognize their limitations, they are able to monitor their parenting accordingly. This makes the emotional outcomes of parenting easier to handle and to understand. The role of parenting is definitely easier for some families than for others.

Here are some of the limiting factors that can influence parenting.

Time management

Parenting takes time. Young children can be demanding. Many parents may find they are unable to juggle the demands of their work pressure with the extra time required for Positive Parenting. Recognizing time as a parenting limitation is something parents need to acknowledge. Once you have admitted that time is a difficult aspect of parenting you will try to find ways to make the time to spend with your child. Parenting with time constraints is not impossible, but working out a tight schedule will lessen the guilt and help parents to manage this time factor.

Temperament

Everyone knows it is part of human nature to have different character traits and different types of temperament. You may be a person with very limited tolerance. A limitation in terms of how much noise you're able to tolerate or how easy it is for you to get down to a little person's level of play would impose limitations on your patience. If temperament is a limitation for you speak with your partner or family members and get some help to give you some time out and space to allow for quality parenting time.

Family dynamics

Every family has different dynamics. Your family may be larger than most or the children may all be little and close in age. You may have a special needs child in the family or perhaps you're a single parent. There are many different family connotations and managing these differences may place parenting limitations on you. Recognizing the limitation enables you to deal with what is lacking and get some help if necessary. Facing up to the limitations pressed on a family in this way, encourages you to make allowances for your circumstances.

Discipline issues

Lack of discipline or too much discipline puts strain on your family relationships. Take a careful look at your parenting discipline style. It may place limitations on your patience. Too strict and you're constantly enforcing the law. Too relaxed and you have no control. Both of these case scenarios will push your patience limitations.

Personal problems

If you're a parent with your own problems of depression, anxiety, anger management, or even personal financial stress, all these factors will place limitations on your patience. It is important for the parents to be looking after themselves and getting help if they have personal problems that may contribute to a lack of patience.

> One moment of patience may ward off great disaster.
>
> One moment of impatience may ruin a whole life.
>
> — ANCIENT CHINESE PROVERB

When you're tempted to be impatient, to shout, criticize, or get really irritable with your child it is time to review your patience threshold. Parents need to be objective and focus on what they can do to interact patiently with their children.

Every family and every individual in that family is unique and different. It takes an objective look at your family and yourself to view what you can control and what you can do with patience.

Take a look at this chart of <u>controlled</u>, patient parenting as opposed to <u>uncontrolled</u> impatient parenting. Where does your parenting style fit in with these different scenarios?

I am in control.	I have lost control.
When I am angry or upset, I can take a pause moment to collect my thoughts.	When I am angry, I immediately react and yell at my child.
I make a point of showing through little things that kindness is important.	I am too busy with work commitments to spend much time thinking of little things to do.
I try to organize a routine at home so everyone can follow instructions easily.	Every day is different. I just hope we muddle through the day and get everything done.
When I make a promise to my child, I keep it realistic and make sure I keep my promises.	I use promises like bribes and sometimes I just don't manage to keep my promises.
Being loyal to my family is very important to me. I honor my family's feelings.	My family is always up to something and I find it helps to gossip about them and share negative stories.
When I am in the wrong, I am not afraid to say I am sorry and build on my relationship with my child.	I am always right. I am the parent, so why should I say I am sorry!
My aim is to foster a win-win situation in my family with a culture of everybody counts and everybody benefits.	I am in charge and everyone must do as I say and follow my orders. The person who wins in our home is the adult person.

Being in control, but not dictatorial, is the basics of positive discipline in Positive Parenting. There are four simple things you can control in every situation.

1. Your voice.
2. Your body language
3. Your ability to be a good listener.

4. The quality time you have available.

These four things will help you gain more control over almost any situation.

1. Your voice:

Speaking with a calm tone of voice and not yelling makes a huge difference to the control you have over any situation. Children tend to switch off when they get shouted at all the time. Take a moment to control your voice. Think about what you say and how you say it. Voice control is a very important factor in being in control of a situation in the teaching world, dealing with young children all the time requires patience and voice control. It is the teacher with the gentle, but firm voice, that commands respect and has the children listening attentively. Children who hear loud shouting voices most of the time tend to give up on listening.

2. Body language:

Body language has an effect on children. Standing over a child with your hands on your hips, as you yell down at them, is harmful to their self-esteem. Try to get down to your child's level when they are little. Use gentle actions not aggressive frightening gestures. Take a moment to pause and have a few deep breaths before reacting with powerful, angry body language.

3. Be a good listener:

Your ability to listen is something you can control. A good listener engages with the person they are listening to. Good listening is about reflective listening. This means you comment appropriately during the conversation. You make comments that are not about I or me, but rather about you. For example, if the conversation is about falling in the garden the listener would reflect empathy by saying you must have felt sad rather than say something about their experiences of falling. In this way the listening skill gives the speaker the chance to share their feelings. The conversation has been about them. It just takes a moment of self-control to practice good listening skills.

4. Quality time:

Everyone is busy. Time constraints affect everyone for different reasons. It could be a high-powered job, or other siblings, or even just the busy life of running your home but with some careful planning and awareness of making time parents can control the time they have available. Quality time is preferable to trying to give a large quantity of time but trying to do too many other things at the same time. Quality time will focus attention on the child. A good way to do this is to have a one-on-one story time or a games time when you make a puzzle together or build with blocks. It is a time when your child has your undivided attention, and you factor that time into your daily routine.

Each of these controllable factors are backed with patience. Patience is the virtue supporting the basic aspects of parenting. It helps to ease situations and to calm parents and children. Is it an easy approach? No, but it is the foundational block to Positive Parenting.

Arnold. H. Glasow, a business and American humorist, described patience and parenting in this way.

"The key to everything is patience.
You get the chicken by hatching the egg, not by smashing it!"

He also said:

"One of the best tests of leadership is the ability to recognize a problem before it becomes an emergency."

How true is this of parenting and guiding your children? In your role as the leaders of your family, one of the great challenges is to recognize negative behavior and put an end to the negative cycle. Negative patterns are harmful to your child. Take a look back in this chapter to recall the table of controlled or uncontrolled behavior. The uncontrolled behavior represents the negative actions that impact in a harmful way towards your child. Look back on the at the behavior that loses control. These are negative behaviors, and it is these behaviors, that with some input from your partner, would need analyzing and positive attention to break the negative cycle.

Ending negative behavior begins with finding your discipline philosophy. This is something you and your parenting partner need to work on. It has to be a team effort and it needs to be planned and prepared. It is not unbending, but it puts your family and the ethos you're trying to create at the forefront of your parenting. The discipline model and the way you follow this as a team makes everything else about Positive Parenting fall in line.

There are several styles of discipline to become familiar with and contemplate carefully. There is never a one size fits all style and parents who are open to modifying their approach will find they grow with the discipline and the family at the same time. Children are growing and learning every day. Developmental milestones come and go and although there may be an underlying factor behind your parenting style, flexibility helps reach goals too.

Here are some parenting styles to consider:

They all differ in their philosophy and a combination may be the right approach for your family. However, it is imperative to agree on the philosophy and to discuss if it is complimenting your family and fitting in with your parenting style.

1. Boundary-based:

A boundary-based discipline sets the boundaries for the behavior expected from the child. Boundary-based discipline is very conscious of consequences. This style of discipline sets clear limits and children know what they are allowed to do. If you cross a boundary there will be a consequence for your actions. Children may well test the limits but when they know the boundary and the consequence, they are less likely to challenge the limits.

Boundary-based discipline requires parents to communicate the limits to the children. It is a good idea for everyone to keep a list of the different boundaries and make your expectations clear to everyone. When a boundary is about to be crossed parents should give a warning and offer choices. The choices will lead to a positive or negative consequence. Parents should try to make these consequences logical. There are natural consequences of children's actions and these revolve around making their own mistakes. Forgetting to pack a sun hat for school could result in having to stay indoors during playtime for example.

2. The Gentle Approach:

This philosophy is based on mutual respect using the teaching aspect of discipline rather than any form of physical punishment. Gentle discipline is similar to Positive Parenting. Children learn respectful negative consequences. Parents try to diffuse bad behavior with what is known as 'When and Then' conditions. There is a great emphasis on safety in this style of parenting. Children are taught what will happen if they do not observe the parenting guidelines. Parents may say:

'When we walk in the car park, we hold hands and then we are not in danger."

Children are made to understand the rules before something happens and they are told what will happen if they break the rules.

3. Positive discipline:

Through this philosophy any misbehavior is used as an opportunity to teach the proper expected behavior. It is a philosophy that aims to develop self-discipline. Teaching the correct behavior at every opportunity. Positive discipline is about taking responsibility and learning problem solving skills. Children cooperate with their parents. Many changes have taken place in society today, in particular both parents are often working parents. Positive discipline nurtures interaction between parents and children with understanding and cooperation.

4. Emotional coaching:

There is an emphasis on feelings through this style of discipline. Children need to learn the skill of empathy. They would have to consider other people's feelings and their win in every situation. The philosophy behind this method of discipline is that everything we do we do with feelings. We are emotionally driven by anger, fear, sadness, joy, and many more feelings. This philosophy requires parents to be involved in teaching children about their feelings. The children will form closer bonds with their parents and deeper friendships. Parents need to find emotional situations to help their children to get in touch with their feelings.

5. Behavior modification:

In this parenting philosophy children learn through their mistakes and modify their behavior accordingly. This technique uses rewards for good behavior and does not support bad behavior. The consequences of good behavior are rewarded. The young child should get rewarded straight away. There are steps to take to enforce behavior modification. This is more a case of positive discipline to change a behavior of a child.

Steps to modify a behavior:

- Asses the child - Age, maturity level, motivations they respond to.
- Asses the behavior – what do you want to modify. Is it just a simple case of remembering to brush their teeth or is it a greater task of putting their toys away neatly?

- Decide on the method – how do you plan to bring about the modification.
- Have a plan – the way you will get the modification done, a plan of action.
- The positive outcome – praise, rewards, privileges awarded when the required behavior is seen.
- Consequences – positive when the modification is working. Negative when the modification is not working.

What kind of discipline style would you choose as a parent? There are multiple factors to consider. It will depend on your lifestyle, the time and patience you have to put in, and the temperament of the child you're trying to discipline. There is a need to be flexible and to put the end goal you have in mind as your ultimate aim. Keep moving forward to this goal. The aim is to use your knowledge of parenting styles and your limitations to practice more patience. Parents can learn some strategies to become more patient.

Here are five suggestions to help you become more patient as a parent. The aim of these suggestions is to help parents implement the discipline style they choose. Parenting is difficult and has stress points to overcome. It is perfectly normal to have some patience threshold and to find you have less patience in some circumstances.

5 ways to help you become a more patient parent.

1. Know your threshold

Everyone has a threshold of pain or in this case of patience. Try to be aware of when that threshold is at its most vulnerable. Is it after a long day at work? Perhaps you're not an early morning person. Do you find dealing with several children's demands at the same time puts pressure on your patience? Everyone has times of the day or situations when they are more likely to lose their patience. Try to identify those times or situations.

2. What is your reaction to the demands on your time

Try to take a moment and think about how you respond. Do you start to feel hot under the collar or irritated with your child? Perhaps you feel a headache coming or you want to yell impatiently. Recognizing the way you respond in situations that rob you of your patience is a way to be in touch with your feelings.

3. Have a management plan

Once you know what sets you off with an impatient response and when and how impatience begins you can work out a strategy to deal with negative feelings of impatience. If your internal switch trips as soon as you get home from work, then plan a few minutes to unwind from work before you begin parenting. Simple calming strategies of deep breathing and consciously keeping calm will help.

4. Sharing is caring

If you know you're having a struggle with personal patience and its limitations, then share your feelings with your parent partner. Share the load of dealing with demanding children when you're able. Discuss strategies to help during the worst times of the day when your patience is limited.

5. Take care of yourself too

There are huge demands on parents these days. Working parents in particular are trying to juggle home responsibilities and work routines. Take time to spoil yourself as a way to recharge your batteries. Personal health care is important and taking time out for yourself is another way to develop patience for the demands of parenting.

Settling on your Positive Parenting philosophy will give you the confidence to finding your feet as a patient parent. There will be adaptions to make and changes to the model of parenting you decide to implement. In fact, without making changes your philosophy will not grow and blend with your family needs.

Our aim as parents is to nurture children to become contributing members of society. The family circle is the starting point. Parenting is about preparation for the wide world.

"We may not be able to prepare the future for our children, but we can at least prepare our children for the future."

— FRANKLIN D ROOSEVELT

Patient parenting in a positive way helps our children to form strong bonds and relationships with the parents they trust. In turn these positive relationships help to prepare children for the future and the part they will play in society.

6

THE STRESS-FREE PARENTING STRATEGIES TO RAISE THE HAPPIEST TODDLER AROUND – GUILT FREE!

There are many philosophies about happiness. Stress-free parenting must be high on the list of happiness for parents. Everyone has a different view of the perfect picture of happiness. Singing is a great way to express happiness.

Children at pre-school love to sing the words to this song:

"If you're happy and you know it clap your hands!"

The song repeats the sentiments of being happy with actions. Stress free parenting would be something to clap and sing about. It is indeed a moment of triumph.

According to a Chinese proverb there are degrees of happiness. They are based on different activities. See how you respond to these degrees of happiness.

Happiness

Happiness for an hour – take a nap.
Happiness for a day – go fishing.
Happiness for a year – inherit a fortune.
Happiness for life – help someone else!
Happiness for a parent - positive parenting!

Knowing stress free parenting strategies that will help you raise a happy toddler will go a long way to reaching this coveted status of raising the happiest toddler. Problems will arise, but it is possible to turn different situations into learning opportunities. The skill is to look objectively at the situation. Then take a moment to turn it into a positive reactive parenting opportunity and follow-up.

Discipline is about teaching and learning, not about punishment. How can parents make discipline learning opportunities? It takes an open mind and an open heart.

Here are some ideas and suggested ways to make discipline a learning opportunity. The secret is to turn the learning opportunity into a game.

Acting out, win an Oscar

When you see an unwanted behavior act it out. Say no to the behavior and then model the right behavior. Have fun with the actions and show your child the behavior you like. Teach your child to applaud the good behavior. You could take this a step further and make an Oscar awards chart. Reward your child with stars on the chart and maybe something special at the end of the week if they have reached a certain number of stars.

Thumbs up, thumbs down

Teach your toddler to make a thumbs up for the good behavior or a thumbs down for the behavior you don't want to continue. Have some fun role modeling the different behaviors and let your toddler give the thumbs up or down sign. Once they have the idea of giving the thumbs up/down sign use it throughout the day.

Statues

Play with a clapping signal. Three loud claps mean freeze like a statue. This can be a good way to reward good behavior. When you see your child doing something good like sitting reading a book or building a puzzle clap three times. Watch them make the statue and then you guess what they are doing, reward the good behavior.

Picture perfect

Make some cards with pictures from magazines. The pictures should show good and bad behavior. Scenes like children being kind. Going to sleep, or playing with friends. These pictures score a thumbs up as you turn them over or deal them out. Have some cards with behavior you think is not to be encouraged like an untidy room or a cross face. These pictures get a thumbs down.

Printable cards are available on the internet and they have all sorts of pictures showing good and bad behavior. Draw a thumbs up or thumbs down sign on each card

If your child is old enough put the cards face down on the table and play a memory game. The idea is to turn up two cards with thumbs up to match while the thumbs down cards are not collected. The winner is the person with the most thumbs up cards. It's all just for fun, but will teach good behavior at the same time.

Simon says

This game is a great copycat game. Play Simon says with your child and they must copy the good, not the bad things you tell them to do.

For example

>*Simon says* brush your teeth.... you brush your teeth.

>*Simon says* chew your nails.... you do not chew your nails.

This is a fun way to talk about things you do not want your child to do.

Sing along

Action songs are a great way to have fun with your toddler and learn good behavior at the same time. The number of action songs available on YouTube will give you many ideas of ways to move to music and learn good behavior. There are old favorites like Here we go round the Mulberry Bush and new rhymes – the list is endless. If your child is going to a playschool, they may come home singing songs and you will be able to learn along with them. Sing anytime and anywhere.

Story time

Story time is the best time of the day. There are many books with stories about being good and doing the right thing. Stories that teach about health and hygiene. Stories to teach about emotions and caring. Books are your number one friend for highlighting good behavior and downsizing bad behavior.

The widely acclaimed children's author Dr Seuss wrote several quotes about books and reading to children. He wrote:

> *"You can find magic wherever you look.*
> *Sit back and relax all you need is.*

And,

> *"You are never too old, too wacky, too wild,*
> *To pick up a book and read to a child.*

His books on health and hygiene are fun to read too.

Look out for Dr Seuss' Sleep Book and The Tooth Book. There is another book called The Things you can do that are good for you. All the Dr Seuss books are cleverly illustrated with pictures children enjoy.

Each of these suggestions, in their own way, help parents to take the disciplinary action they wish to take and turn it into a game. It is fun activities like these that help their children understand what good behavior is all about. Good behavior is commended over and above bad or undesirable behavior.

Find the gap!

Look objectively at the undesirable behavior. Perhaps it is caused by a gap in your child's development or a delay in their growth milestones. The gap, or delay could be the root cause of the improper or frustrated behavior. Developmental milestones are very key parts of where your child may be functioning. A temper tantrum for example may be born out of a gap or a lack of some kind of skill your child has yet to acquire. When your child has a meltdown moment over some activity, they have failed to perform have a look at your expectations. Ask yourself if your child could actually manage to perform the task they set out to finish.

Here are some scenarios you may be experiencing. Ask yourself if your child has the skills, mental and physical, to complete the task you're expecting them to complete. Milestones are part of physical, cognitive, social, and emotional development as well as communication. Reaching a milestone enables a child to complete certain tasks. Parents who are aware of these milestones will be able to understand why a child may not be able to perform some of the activities. The knowledge of milestones and what a child should be able to do will help parents to fill the gap, if there is one, because of a developmental delay.

There are high expectations for children as they start school earlier and find themselves trying to be independent earlier. Here are some examples of the skills children may be expected to learn:

- Tying shoelaces,
- Packing away books and toys,
- Using a knife and fork,
- Getting dressed,
- Coloring neatly.

These may be some of the activities toddlers struggle with as they start becoming more independent. Look for other ways to achieve the same outcome. Velcro instead of laces is a wonderful way to do up shoes before your child has the fine motor skills to cope with laces. Using a spoon and fork before using the full regalia of table cutlery helps to introduce children to cutlery when they are still learning to eat independently. Pull on pull off clothing to avoid fiddly buttons and big chunky crayons for the early stages of learning how to color.

There are many ways to filter into independence and becoming self-reliant.

Toddlers, tantrums, and trying behavior may be the result of your toddler's frustration because they are unable to manage some of the tasks they have been given and added to their frustration is the fact that they do not have the communication to tell you why they are stamping their feet and yelling right now!

Jerry Seinfeld once said:

> *"Having a two-year-old is kind of like having a blender, but you don't have a top for it!"*

This stage of development is often known as the terrible twos. One of the most noticeable behaviors of the terrible two-year-old is the tantrum they can throw when they lose their patience and self-control. The frenzied behavior is difficult to stop and exasperating for parents. One of the things that sets the two-year-old off down a path of terrible behavior is having to wait for something. It could be waiting for something to happen or for someone to arrive or for the chance to go outside and play. Toddlers do not play the waiting game well. They do not have the maturity to wait patiently.

What can you do to avoid a negative outcome from having to wait?

Toddlers do not have the patience to wait for things to happen. They can probably sit and wait for about two minutes. They do not have the ability to develop patience and delay gratification in different circumstances. Waiting is not one of their games. The best way to wait for an event is to be prepared. There are times when waiting cannot be avoided. However, if you're aware that waiting is going to be a problem and that waiting is not something your toddler can do easily then you can be prepared.

Think ahead

Don't make appointments that clash with your toddlers needs like mealtimes or sleep times. A tired and hungry person is going to be more difficult.

Be prepared

If you know the waiting time is going to take a while be prepared with a bag of distractions. A few toys and a couple of books will make the world of difference. Add in a snack and something to drink and you will have hunger pains sorted.

Give praise

Make sure you praise the good behavior so then your child will know what you enjoyed and why it was good.

Developing communication skills, as you interact with a toddler, is a key factor in stress free parenting. Communication is a vital part of Positive Parenting and it helps with understanding your child as well as bringing another dimension to your relationship.

Here are 5 ways to develop your young child's communication skills.

1. Speak to your child slowly, clearly, and often. The more you talk to them the more they will hear and imitate you.
2. Look at picture books and point out the picture followed by the word to describe the picture. Make use of themed books like animals, the farm or the sea to build up vocabulary.
3. Talk about experiences yours and theirs. *(For example, fetch the ball and give it to me.)*
4. Play fantasy games. Have a tea party for example or pretend to go shopping.
5. Play 'I Spy' or simple card games. The more you speak about

things around you the more vocabulary your child will develop.

Children's language development moves forward at a rapid rate from the age of two till three. Look at the huge jump from two to three years of age.

Age two:

children can follow some simple directions and say about fifty new words. They have the ability to combine a few words into a phrase. They can follow a simple two step instruction. For example, 'Fetch the ball and give it to me.'

Age three:

Their vocabulary has increased to 200 or more words. They can put together three- or four-word sentences. Three-year-olds understand more and their speech is clearer. A parent can usually understand about 75% of what the child is saying.

Communication problems you may notice need to be checked. Look out for hearing problems, delayed speech, difficulty following directions, stuttering, or unclear speech. The earlier problems are detected and attended to the better.

Positive communication skills are one of the most important parenting tools. Taking time to encourage your child to learn to speak, develop their vocabulary, and start to express their feelings is the beginnings of a growing relationship.

Making and sharing mealtimes together is one of the most important ways to develop connectivity with a child. When everyone is sitting at the table give every family member an opportunity to say something about their day. Giving and receiving praise is a very vital way to build a communication bond.

A morning and an evening routine are great ways to start and end the day together. It does not have to be a lengthy chunk of time, just something you do together. A walk in the garden, playing with a pet, washing face and brushing hair and teeth routine are some of the suggestions of activities to do together to start the day. In the evening have your bath and supper routine mapped out. Include a bedtime story and nighttime prayers to bless our friends and family. These are all good communication skills and ways to bond with your child.

Exercising together with a walking schedule or perhaps you and your child may enjoy doing some yoga or swimming or playing with a ball. Take the dog for a walk or go to the park and exercise on the equipment there. Doing something physical is very positive and good for building relationships.

Spending some time together in the kitchen preparing a meal or making cookies encourages positive communication. Try making something to share with the family. It could be a batch of biscuits or cupcakes. Decorating the cakes or biscuits and sharing them with the family is a positive way to do something together and to share the spoils with another member of the family.

Get down to your child's level and just enjoy these quality times together.

This concept may be a little more challenging if you have a special needs child in your family. There will be concerns about how to handle communication and discipline. Parents will be wanting to know how to incorporate positive parenting and family discipline into their routine. Showing and sharing love with your special needs child is the key to developing your special relationship. Your special needs child will have different milestones to reach and different developmental stages. However, discipline, as in training and teaching, will be important. Special needs children need routine and boundaries to feel safe and secure.

The following guidelines are not rigid parenting rules and do not take into account the differences between the many types of special needs areas and the best approach for each special need according to the physical, cognitive, social, and emotional needs. They are simply guidelines to acknowledge special needs and assist with some general parenting ideas to reach the goal of being a positive parent in all circumstances.

Training, teaching and developing discipline styles for special needs children:

1. Demonstrate love and kindness with a gentle spirit over all circumstance.
2. Be consistent. Special needs children need to know you will react consistently and that they can depend on you.
3. Learn as much as you can about your child disability. Speak to doctors, specialists, care givers, special schools,

psychologist and behaviorists who may be involved with supporting you and your child.
4. Have a definite idea of acceptable and not acceptable behavior within the limits of your child's ability.
5. Have consequences with rewards for desired behavior.
6. Communicate in clear simple messages with the right expectations.
7. Routines are very important to special needs children. Have a routine set up that helps your child through strategic times of the day. Mealtimes for example.
8. Be patient. Patience will be high on the demands list to create an emotional bond with your special needs child.
9. Create a safe home space for your special needs child so they can feel secure.
10. Have confidence in yourself and seek help and advice from specialists.
11. Be ready to make changes whenever necessary.
12. Take time out for yourself.
13. Keep believing in your special needs child and praise small victories all the time.
14. Remember discipline is about guidance not punishment.
15. Give clear instructions and build on what can be done, taking small steps at a time based on your knowledge of your child.

While embracing a special needs child in the family remember to praise and show compassion. Your child will be overcoming larger obstacles than your normal child. Lavishing love and patient understanding, with secure boundaries will lead the way to positive parenting with a special needs child.

Special needs children have overcome great obstacles in life. Their abilities to shine on the sports field and in society give everyone hope and encouragement.

Helen Keller gave everyone these words of wisdom and a key to happiness.

"Your success and happiness lies in you. Resolve to keep happy and your joy and you shall form an invincible host against difficulties."

Helen Keller, who lost her sight at the age of eighteen months, became an author, disability rights advocate, political activist, and lecturer.

The power of positive parenting lies in these words too. Keeping patient and positive and nurturing success and happiness will help parents enjoy stress free parenting with a large measure of happiness.

7

SEEKING PROFESSIONAL HELP

Parenting and raising children is bound to bring different challenges and problems. At what point do you as a parent look for professional help. Is it wise to reach out for input from a professional or should you stick with what you know? Could you hope to find a solution through your own experience and knowledge?

Abraham Maslow, American psychologist and creator of Maslow's hierarchy of needs, had this to say:

> *"If the only tool you have is a hammer; you tend to see every problem as a nail."*

Parents are by no means limited to the kind of help they can reach for. There is no need to bash away at one form of therapy or source of help. Finding the right help may actually be overwhelming. There are many tools in the parenting toolbox and different ways to find the right kind of help. Parenting and solving problems is not limited to one method or one resource.

Where do you begin if you're concerned?

Start by looking within. Try some good housekeeping methods as you look in-house at the problems you're facing.

Here are some ideas of indicators that you may have a problem...

- What difficulties are you experiencing and are they getting worse?
- Do some of these difficulties qualify as just normal growing pains, or could they be more serious?
- Are you finding the difficulties are becoming more frequent?
- Are the unwanted behaviors occurring in different places at different times?
- Have you tried all your particular ways of getting to resolve the problem, but nothing is working?
- Do you feel out of control and concerned about the behaviors?

Before you rush off to the nearest specialist it may be helpful to read through some of the common problems that affect most children at some time or other. When these problems get out of hand, or you as a parent feel they are problematic, then an assessment with a pediatrician could help you to find the right specialist for treatment and advice, or behavior modification.

Here are 10 common behavior problems that may affect many children:

1. Having a defiant attitude: Do you feel this defiance is more than normal?

It is normal for children to say 'No' sometimes and try to push their boundaries. Do you feel this defiance is more than normal?

2. Problems with eating the right food

Try to be proactive towards developing good eating habits. Make sure your child is not taking food at the wrong time and then will not be happy at supper time.

3. Spending too much time of watching TV or using electronic devices

These devices may become addictive. Knowing when to stop watching is important and monitoring channels is part of keeping an eye on a possible problem with electronic devices.

4. Lying

Understanding why children lie is an important factor. Children lie to get out of perceived trouble, to get more attention, or to start feeling better about themselves.

5. Showing disrespect to others

Calling people names or throwing things at them is not respectful. Try ignoring disrespectful behavior.

6. Impulsive behavior

Young children are very likely to show impulsive behavior. They may hit one another or shout out things without thinking. Impulsive behavior can be corrected by encouraging thinking skills and changes may come about with maturity.

7. Poor sleeping habits

Bedtimes can be very challenging, and a bedtime routine is one of the best ways to establish a good sleep habits. Consistency is a vital part of establishing a bedtime routine.

8. Aggression

Frustration is usually the root cause of aggression. It could be that your child does not have the words yet to say how they feel or the dexterity to get what they want. Toddlers may have bouts of aggression born out of frustration. Make sure you teach your child how to make amends for any aggression that may have hurt someone.

9. Impulsive behavior

Acting without thinking is a problem for younger children. You may need to teach impulse control skills. When you see this does not help the behavior problem praise the good behavior of exercising self-control.

10. Temper tantrums

Tantrums are associated with the 'Terrible Twos' the difficult toddler stage. They can be part of the behavior of older children's behavior. Most tantrums should just be ignored unless they could cause harm.

These are part of normal behavior problems and can usually be addressed at home or as part of preschool interventions or new routines. However, if you feel uncomfortable or concerned about any of these issues get advice or set up an appointment to see a specialist.

Preschool difficulties.

When Your child enters the preschool environment, you will have an opportunity to discuss problem areas with a qualified preschool teacher. Always be open with your child's teacher about any problems you may be experiencing. It is very likely that your child is manifesting the same difficulties at school and your child's teacher will help you seek professional advice.

The preschool environment may give early warning signs of a learning disability. Attending to any difficulties as early as possible is a key to discovering developmental delays or learning disabilities. Children do develop at different paces and even in the same family the differences may be noticeable. The important factor is to remember that early intervention can make all the difference to social and academic development.

The following areas are ones to watch and investigate should you feel there is a problem in consultation with your child's teacher. There are suggested milestones that will help parents to decide on seeking professional help.

Look thoroughly at the following developmental areas:

Language development

Do you feel your child is acquiring vocabulary, asking questions, and interacting with you? A three-year-old should have an estimated vocabulary of 200 words and be able to name some body parts and everyday objects. If you have a concern in the language area it could be there is a hearing loss or an auditory processing disorder. Chronic ear infections can cause language delays.

Immaturity

Does your child act very babyish or show signs of immaturity? There can be a number of reasons for social immaturity. Children will struggle to make the transition to more formal education without the right level of social maturity. The preschool teachers will have plenty of experience in determining children's maturity levels.

Gross and fine motor delays

Your preschool teacher will soon advise you of any motor difficulties. Gross motor being large movements and playing on the outdoor equipment. Fine motor difficulties associated with holding a pencil or handling smaller objects like building blocks.

Inappropriate behavior with other children

Aggressive behavior, anti-social behavior, and lack of cooperation would all signal some form of poor social skills and the school may suggest seeking specialist advice.

Destructive behavior

The school will soon call you to discuss destructive behavior. Children can be rough with toys but there is a difference between being heavy handed and being destructive. Children with anger issues, and compulsive behavior may need to be seen by a behaviorist.

Parents need to dig deep into the toolbox of ways to overcome problems. There are many different 'tools' available and seeking the help of a specialist is just one of the ways to get help for your parenting problems. There is no shame attached to reaching out for some professional help and guidance.

L R. Knost, an award-winning author, and founder and director of Children's Rights Advocacy has many encouraging sayings about gentle parenting. Looking at childhood as a precious time of a child's life she says:

> "Instead of raising children who turn out okay,
> **despite their childhood**,
> Let's raise children who turn out extra ordinary,
> **because of their childhood.**"

Seeking the advice of a professional could make all the difference to your child's childhood experiences. Problems do not have to stop children from having a happy and successful childhood.

There are many specialists available and a good place to start is with the doctors and specialists you will come into contact for most of the basic needs of your child. A family doctor or pediatrician could be the starting point for specialist intervention, so it is a good idea to have a family doctor or pediatrician you trust and build up a relationship with them.

Here is a list of the basic medical practitioners most families refer to.

Family doctor or Pediatrician

Choosing a family doctor, GP, or a pediatrician is a personal choice. Both these medical practitioners will perform your child's annual medical exam, treat common illness and manage inoculations for childhood illness. While children are very young most families choose to have a pediatrician to manage health care issues. Later in your child's development you will switch to a family doctor. The family doctor or pediatrician is the best starting point if you feel there is a medical problem you need to sort out.

Dentist, or Pediatric dentist

Dental hygiene is very important and having a dentist form an early age will help you with the challenges of any dental problems. The dentist will take x-rays to ensure healthy teeth are waiting to arrive in your child's mouth and refer you to an orthodontist if there is a need.

Getting your child used to visiting the dentist and co-operating in the dentist chair is a good health habit.

Optometrist or ophthalmologist

Your child's first eye exam will take place at birth. The doctor who delivers the baby will inspect the child's eyes and how they respond to light. As your child grows up and you can observe more of their visionary needs if you suspect a problem then you would consult an optometrist or an ophthalmologist. Both of these specialists are referred to as eye doctors but the ophthalmologist is the specialist who can perform operations while the optometrist prescribes corrective glasses. Your child may be referred by the school or their class teacher for eye problems. Children should have regular eye examinations because a pair of corrective glasses will make all the difference to their school performance.

Other specialists for physical problems may be needed to help with issues like allergies, hormones, and metabolic issues, skin problems and ear, nose, and throat disorders. Your pediatrician will refer you to any of these specialists depending on the problem.

Allergist

Allergic reactions can be very disturbing especially if they are the underlying cause of conditions like asthma. The allergist will check your child for allergic reactions to different substances or natural elements they may be allergic to. Finding out what your child is sensitive to will help with voicing anything that cause an allergic reaction. Further intervention may lead you to an ENT, ear, nose, and throat specialist.

Endocrinologist

The endocrinologist is a specialist who looks at the production of hormones and the body's metabolism. If your child has diabetes or a hormone imbalance or trouble with their thyroid or adrenal system, the endocrinologist is the specialist to see. Thyroid and adrenal problems are unlikely to occur until children get closer to puberty.

Dermatologist

Your family doctor or pediatrician will refer you to a dermatologist for any skin problems. These would include inherited skin disorders and birthmarks. Severe rashes and skin irritations may also fall under allergies.

Mental health and the behavioral status of your child leads parents to another form of health care with another set of specialists. Mental health is a very important part of health care and through specialist intervention parents can find answers and help for various mental health issues. Mental health can be much harder to deal with because it is not visible. Mental health issues are seen through behavior patterns and it takes different specialists to intervene for different mental disabilities.

Some disabilities are behavioral while others are cognitive or genetic. All children deserve to have an accurate diagnosis and the correct support and intervention for these disorders.

Teachers and care workers will be the first to alert parents to poor school performance or not being able to reach the acceptable milestones. Mental health care embraces many different specialists and different methods of treatment. This is an overview of some of the specialists and forms of treatment. Everything will depend on the health issue, the age of the child, and other circumstances. It is comforting to know there are specialists available to make yours and your child's problems easier to handle.

Pediatric psychiatrist and psychologists

These specialists work closely together for the emotional needs of children. The process of helping children needing assistance with mental health issues will begin with an assessment and some psychological testing. There may be a need for medical assistance and psychotherapy. Deciding on the right therapy and support program starts with this interview and exam.

Mental health conditions cover a wide variety of concerns. Anxiety, depression, coping with stress. Eating disorders, behavior management, post-traumatic stress, and obsessive-compulsive disorders may be part of a mental illness. Children may need testing if they are possibly on the autism spectrum or have ADD issues and ADHD problems. All these mental issues can be detected by an assessment and then the child will get professional help. It probably sounds very scary to be facing mental health issues, but with specialist intervention there is at least support and direction to follow.

Counselors and different therapists in talk therapy or play therapy help overcome many of the mental health issues. Support groups are great therapy units to help with every condition especially with coping with some of the more specific syndromes and disorders.

Partnering with a therapist or a support group gives parents the confidence they need to deal with physical and mental health issues. Finding the balance is a really important factor in dealing with these issues. You do not have to feel you're the hammer in Abraham's Maslow's toolbox. Join up with others to get support along the way of your parenting journey.

Bringing up a healthy happy child is perhaps a bit of a balancing act. You may want to see yourself as a facilitator. Here are some suggestions to help towards bringing up a healthy happy child. They involve mental, physical, and social aspects of growing up.

Coupled with positive parenting, you should find some answers to the ideal of having a happy healthy child.

12 TIPS TO FOSTER HEALTHY HAPPY CHILDREN

1. Be a good listener

Listening is a really vital parenting skill. Children need to feel you're giving them your undivided attention. When you listen to children giving them your full attention you can read their body language and hear what they are saying.

2. Embrace the outdoors

Spending time appreciating fresh air and enjoying the beauty of nature is another aspect of growing up that helps create happiness

3. Make time for play opportunities

Children learn through play. Playing imaginative games or building with blocks and construction toys are all part of happy growing up times.

4. Don't make unfair comparisons

Respect that each of your children are unique and have their own strengths. Never make unfair comparisons.

5. Help children to be in touch with their feelings

Recognizing feeling helps children to adjust to their emotions and deal with anger and negative feelings as well as happy feelings.

6. Make happy memories together

Memories make up family traditions and as children grow up their family memories will help them through tough times and build on their happy feelings.

7. Encourage all kinds of efforts

Always motivate children through your encouraging words. Words of affirmation are important to build self-esteem and confidence.

8. Give them some responsibilities

Children need to be given responsibilities starting with small tasks around the house or keeping their own things in good order. Responsibility and taking care of possessions makes for positive feelings about the good things you have.

9. Have healthy eating and exercise habits

Correct eating habits and making sure your child gets exercise helps to keep the body and the mind positive and happy.

10. Monitor screen time

Everything in moderation they say, and this is true for the time spent watching TV. It is a good idea to monitor what your child is watching and block out violent and aggressive programs. They are not conducive to feeling happy.

11. Praise sincere efforts

Children thrive on praise. Make it sincere praise for something well done and show appreciation for acts of kindness.

12. Be happy yourself

Part and parcel of encouraging happiness is being happy within yourself. Make time for some personal time and to do something that feels good for you to encourage your own happy state of being.

Above all be grateful for what you have and show gratitude to others for what they bring to your life on a daily basis. An attitude of gratitude goes a long way towards happiness.

III

LET'S TALK ABOUT POTTY TRAINING

We are going to kick off this section of this book with a quick overview of potty training.

When the time comes are you ready for this and is your child ready to be trained?

Our potty-training guide covers a program based on -

TIME to train your toddler to use the POTTY!

1. **T** time ……… when is the best time?
2. **I** interesting… facts to learn about this phase
3. **M** mentally…. preparing for this event
4. **E** equipping … yourself for the best journey

……... to start to train your toddler to use the…

- **P** potty……….. planned play begins.
- **O** overnight…a challenging step
- **T** toddler…….carers need to be a support
- **T** totally……... understanding commitment
- **Y** you win…….yes to success.

So, let's launch into this section of the book.…...

WHEN IS THE BEST TIME TO START POTTY TRAINING?

TIME

Timing is one of the keys to success. Finding the right time does not only depend on time, but it is also part and parcel of readiness. Your toddler needs to have reached a readiness level in several areas of development. Based on individual growth and maturity, this time could vary for toddlers. Finding the best or the right time depends on several different factors. Child developmental experts will agree a good time to start is between 18 months and 3 years. During that time observe your child and monitor these developmental areas indicating readiness to start learning how to use the potty.

Emotional readiness:

Is your child showing a desire to be more independent? Does your toddler want to do things for himself or herself? Emotional readiness is a contributor to being ready for potty training. This is a time when your child becomes more aware of listening and responding to you.

Physical readiness:

Can your child sit by themselves and balance on a potty or toilet seat, if you choose a child's toilet training seat? Using the potty successfully is part of learning different skills. It follows on from sitting, crawling, standing and walking. Successful potty training is interlinked with your toddler being able to support themselves on the potty and being able to get to the potty. Initially there will be some parental help, but ultimately the toddler needs to reach the potty independently.

Social readiness:

Will your toddler respond to some simple instructions and be able to sit for a short while? Can your child look at books or engage with you as you go about training them for the routine of potty training? Does your toddler show an interest in what goes on in the bathroom? You may have to give up some of your privacy as your toddler is curious about what happens in the bathroom. Encourage little games with toys pretending to go to the toilet. All these activities help children become aware of using the toilet and cooperating with toilet training.

Martin Luther King said:

> *"The time is always right to do what is right."*

However, with potty training, starting too early or when the right signs are not there, your training program could go badly. Starting too early, before your child is ready, can have repercussions and end up causing delays.

It would be better, with potty training, to have the mindset that tells you...

You can do what is right when the time is right.

Feeling that the time is right to start potty training is helped by checking these milestones or developmental stages. Ask yourself these questions to decide if the time is right or if you need some more time before you and your child are ready for potty training and all that goes with this big milestone.

Are you beginning to see signs of independence?

Your toddler wants to try and dress themselves. Putting their shoes on back to front, and saying 'me do' are indications of wanting some independence. Trying to feed themselves and sit on grown up chairs show you your child is keen to grow up and become independent. The inevitable NO, and defiant attitude during the two-year-old phase, shows you that attitude of wanting to be in charge. These are the signs you're looking for.

Is your toddler showing an interest in the bathroom?

Every time you go to the bathroom a little person follows you and wants to know what you're doing. They will happily wash their hands as you do and may pretend to go to the potty. Some toddlers delight in unraveling the toilet roll and dragging it across the room. Your toddler is interested in the bathroom.

Do you notice your toddler is dry for longer?

Noticing the length of time between dry and wet diapers is helpful. You may feel adventurous and leave the diaper off while your toddler plays in the garden. Take note of when there is a bowel movement and if there is a pattern to the times of day that these happen. These are indicators that there is more control for these bodily functions.

Will your toddler manage to pull on and take off training pants?

Part of the training involves pulling on training pants. When your child starts to dress themselves, they will start to put on their own undies. It is much easier to potty train when your toddler can manage this skill. It will help them get to the potty in time and organize themselves. When your toddler is able to take their undies off, they may also be ready to have a better sense of needing to go to the potty. There will come a time when your child can manage to go to the bathroom and use the potty independently.

Can your toddler start to follow simple directions?

Does your toddler have the ability to listen to simple instructions like stand up or sit down? Can your toddler remember the pee and poop words you have chosen? Will your toddler call you if they need help? These are all signs of improved communication and maturity.

Has your child reached the physical milestones of sit, stand, and walk?

Is your toddler fairly mobile and steady in a sitting position? Can your toddler walk to the potty and sit on it for a few minutes? If your child is still learning these physical growth milestones, it would not be wise to introduce another skill to manage with learning to sit on the potty.

Can your toddler sit still for a short period of time?

Sitting on the potty and managing to urinate or pass a bowel movement needs some length of time. Your toddler needs to be able to sit in the right position on the potty or the toddler toilet seat. If your child is not able to sit still for a short while, then sitting on the potty is going to prove difficult. It would be better to have some practice sessions with no expectations for a while. Toddlers are able to turn potty time into times of manipulation and power struggles. This is something to be wary of if you start training before your child is ready. They may decide to use this activity as a way to gain psychological power over you.

Can your toddler communicate using a few simple words?

There needs to be an element of communication between you and your child. You should ask yourself if you're able to attract your toddler's attention and manage to sit them on the potty for a short while. Are you able to distract your toddler from what they are doing to come and sit on the potty? That is an indication that you may be able to start a toilet routine.

Is your toddler happy to comply with the potty routine?

Part of potty training involves hand washing and keeping clean after using the potty. Your toddler will need to follow directions to complete the potty routine. Do you think your child is ready for listening to your simple instructions and starting to follow a routine in the bathroom?

Do you notice bowel movements are becoming more regular?

Once your child is eating more routine solid meals, and fitting into a daily pattern of eating and sleeping times, there should be evidence that bowel movements are becoming more regular. This is an indication for you that your child could be put on the potty at regular times during the day. It is more likely that they would be able to perform on the potty. Getting to this regular stage helps your child to know the signs that indicate a need to go and sit on the potty.

Do you see signs that your child does not like wearing a dirty diaper?

When children start to tell their parents they have dirtied their diaper or they feel messy and indicate they don't like this feeling they are ready to start using the potty. Training pants often help with feeling the sensation of messing because, unlike a diaper, the process of a bowel movement can be felt. At this stage many toddlers will stop what they are doing to report they have messed their pants.

Watching out for all these signs is important and a contributing factor to readiness to start using the potty. However, many parents ask if there is a recommended age. How old should a toddler be to start potty training? While there are guidelines there is no hard and fast rule like a due date or a Ready steady go formula. The reason for this is every child is such an individual in every way! Putting a name and a date to any bodily function, or developmental milestone, is not possible.

There are suggested readiness dates and possible norms, but as a parent it is really difficult to set the clock for 'Potty Training Day.' The most important contribution to choosing a date is your child's signals of being ready to start toilet training.

Here are some 6 monthly intervals you may consider to start training. Look at the possible scenario at each age level and process the theory at that level. Would it suit your child and your lifestyle to start training in any of these intervals?

Age 0 – 12 months. Known as Infant Potty Training.

This sounds very foreign to many parents. In places like India, China, and East Africa parents learn to recognize the signal from their infant that they are ready to eliminate. The parent holds the infant over the designated place and as the child passes urine or has a bowel movement the parent makes a sound that will in time be associated with going to the toilet. Obviously the infant and parent need to be together all the time for this to work initially.

Age 12 – 18 months. Older infants and young toddlers.

This was a popular phase to start during the 1920's and 1930's babies were in cloth diapers and mothers were very hands on with their children. The trend today is to wait longer. Toddlers are very active at this age. They are learning to walk and explore. They are too busy finding out about their world to want to sit on a potty. You may want to try at this stage, but be guided by your child's developmental milestones.

Age 18 – 24 months. Watch for toilet readiness signs.

This seems to be a popular age to get started if you feel your toddler is ready. Look out for the readiness signs and decide if your child is ready. One of the most important signs is a desire to become more independent and a growing awareness of the physical signs of going to the toilet. If your child is not cooperative at this stage it is best not to force the issue and end up with a power struggle between you.

Older than 24 months.

Around 24 months seems to be a popular time to start potty training. Studies have shown children learn quicker at this age. Starting to toilet train much later can result in incontinence problems. Children who have not learned to control the flow of urine through training to use the potty may experience difficulties with urine control.

Another consideration for the starting time should be your child's health. A child with no bowel problems, like diarrhea or constipation, is going to have a better experience starting to use the potty. A relaxed child without emotional stress will also find the transition to the potty easier. Finally, a child who is ready to cooperate will have a better more positive experience.

There is no hard and fast rule of a starting time. The majority of families like to start around the two-year mark. Sooner or later, it will be the parent's decision of when to start, based on their knowledge of the process, and the signs that their child is ready.

Should you decide to start earlier and try the Infant Training Method you will need to be close to your child all the time to work with their needs. The Infant Training Method would not suit working moms, it is a very time-consuming training method. It does have the advantage of not needing diapers and rashes are avoided. The Infant Training Method builds a very strong bond between mother and child.

Starting much later has other considerations because there is a medical concern about incontinence and lack of motivation to become more independent. A late starter may be teased by their peers and find themselves anxious because they are different. Many play schools or preschools prefer children to come to school diaper free.

There is a time for everything. A time and a season. Each child will be ready at different times and in different seasons. The best time is the time that both you and your toddler feel ready to begin. Using potty training books with guidelines and encouragement will help you find the right time for you and your toddler. Being prepared and confident as a parent is just as important in the timing part of potty training.

Review these preparation time ideas and take some time to feel prepared.

- Take time to build up to potty training with talking about the potty.
- Make time to read some books with funny potty stories.
- Dispel the myth of potty training as some big problem that is difficult to overcome.
- Set aside some time to get the potty area in the bathroom ready. This indicates to your toddler there is a time coming when they will be using the potty.
- Find time to ask your toddler about the potty. Then judge by

your toddlers reactions to your conversations if they interested enough to begin to use the potty?
- Timing and having enough time to devote to the training is important. It is not advisable to start potty training before a big family event, moving house, another baby is due to arrive, or your child is changing schools. Major events are unsettling and not a good time to start.

Think about the direction you're going in and the end goal. It has been said that:

"People often complain about lack of time when lack of direction is the real problem."

According to Zig Ziglar, American author and motivational speaker.

The chapters following this one will give you direction and motivation to get the timing right and have potty training success.

9

DECIPHERING THE FACTS, AND CLEARING UP THE MISCONCEPTIONS OF POTTY TRAINING

INTERESTING:

Yes, as a parent starting out to potty train your toddler you will find there are interesting myths and misconceptions. Perhaps you have heard some of them before, but now you're potty training, you wonder if there is some truth in the myths.

"The enemy of the truth is very often not the lie, deliberately contrived and dishonest but the myth, persistent, persuasive, and unrealistic."

— JOHN F KENNEDY

Myths and legends can become such a part of our belief system, handed down over the years, that they soon become what we consider a truth. How many of these myths have you heard and how many of them sound true to you?

Let's dispel the myths.

Myth #1 – Starting to potty train too soon can cause with-holding urine and constipation.

Fact - It is not how soon you start the process. Potty training depends on a number of factors including readiness to start using a potty or toilet seat. The right time depends on each individual child. However, there are physical milestones and once they are reached, sitting on the potty and knowing what is manageable. This has nothing to do with possible urine or constipation issues.

Myth #2 - Your child will decide when it is the right time to start.

Fact – Your toddler will let you know through his/her interest in the potty and using the bathroom. Parents need to nurture an interest in the potty and help teach their toddler the necessary skills. Showing an interest is just part of the readiness process. Parents need to be ready to start the training process too. It is training because you're going to teach your toddler how to do something they don't know how to do. Your child may show an interest but that does not mean they are telling you this is the day we will start potty training.

Myth #3 – The children's day care center will do the training.

Fact – There needs to be teamwork with input from your side as well as the daycare. Some daycare facilities like the children to be potty trained before they are accepted. Liaise with your caregivers and fit into their routine so together you reach a potty-trained toddler. The positive factor of daycare training is children do learn from each other. All the little people in your child's group will be using the toilet during toilet time. The toilets and facilities are child friendly and this is an added factor to consider when children are at a daycare facility. Daycare certainly helps the process, but parents should buy into the process too.

Myth #4 – Boys are harder to train than girls.

Fact – Readiness to use the potty or to start training is an individual milestone. It is not related to gender. Boys may appear less interested in keeping clean, but they may get the idea of how things work quicker. Girls may want to be clean and neat and find using the bathroom a desirable part of their routine. It is not possible to generalize and attribute a slow start to the gender of the child.

Myth #5 – Starting too soon upsets the bladder.

Fact – The bladder is a muscle it is not affected by early use. What is important to note is that by 2 – 3 years of age your child has more control over the muscles around the bladder. The sphincter and pelvic floor muscles are stronger and can hold back the urine. The bladder is able to hold more urine by the age of 2 – 3.

Myth #6 – Accidents after you have potty trained mean you have failed.

Fact – There are bound to be accidents or signs of regression. Your child may be feeling emotional about something and have an accident. Perhaps your toddler is engrossed in an activity and forgets to go and use the potty. It does not mean you have failed. Be patient and understanding and carry on with the routine if possible.

Myth #7 - Pull ups do not help with the process of potty training.

Fact – Pull ups have their place, but because they are similar in a way to a diaper with absorbent materials, your toddler may not feel the sensation of relieving themselves. They will not associate what happens when you need to go to the potty and what happens if you have an accident. Pull ups can be used as an interim measure, but because they are very similar in the materials they use to be absorbent, they do feel more like a diaper. Training with undies or training pants is often more effective then pull ups.

Myth #8 - Potty training is a wonderful time of bonding and building relationships.

Fact – Potty training is hard work and accidents will happen. Potty training takes patience and understanding as well as perseverance. It is a time of consistent motivation and every day may not lead to happy bonding time. The experience depends on many factors so it may not necessarily be a perfect bonding time.

Myth #9 - Excited applause and big rewards are essential to get potty training right.

Fact – While some rewards are good it is important to avoid over rewarding or clapping and cheering excessively. This puts pressure on your child to perform for you every time they sit on the potty. The praise is best when it is just a matter of fact well done and not a whole chorus of cheering and applause. Reward charts work well when your child is old enough to understand.

Asking and answering questions is an important part of understanding how children learn to use the potty and more often than not parents are asking the same questions.

FAQ's to help clear up myths and misunderstandings about potty training.

Here are 10 of the most frequently asked questions answered for you.

#1. Are there differences in the way you potty train a boy or a girl?

A. The introductions to potty training and the readiness application are pretty much the same except the anatomy is different. Potty training is a little more complicated for boys. The difference is obviously due to the natural differences between boys and girls. It is a good idea to start the same way with boys sitting initially to pass urine. When boys are ready to stand and wee like a big brother or dad the process changes and is a little more complicated. Boys have to learn how to aim their penis in the right direction and if they need to have a bowel movement then they must change from a standing position to a sitting position. Take the steps through from sitting to standing and aiming in the potty to standing and aiming in the toilet just like dad. Be sure to provide a step to make everything easy and comfortable for your son. Get dad involved to provide the extra male support.

#2. What is the age that most children learn to use the potty?

A. Generally speaking, children learn to use the potty around the two-year-old stage. However, there is no set time or specific date for potty training it is very dependent on each child's individual readiness for this activity. Control and willingness to go to the potty in the day generally happens between the age of two-to-three years of age. Control through the night may only be reached between the ages of 3-to-4 and a half years of age.

#3. Should I be worried if my child has been dry for a while and then starts having accidents?

A. Accidents or some regression can happen. It may be a reaction to some sort of stress. Things like moving house, starting a new school, the arrival of another baby, or an unusual event in the family. There are many kinds of incidents that could trigger an accident. Try to figure out what it is and offer love, patience, and reassurance as you get back on track.

#4. Can children go straight to using the toilet and not use a potty?

A. Choosing to use a potty or the toilet is entirely up to you and your child. Some children feel more secure on the potty with their feet on the ground. Other children are happy to use a toilet seat on the main toilet. There are some very user-friendly toilet seats for toddlers. Choose one that suits your needs and provide a step up to help your toddler reach the seat.

#5. At what age in the toilet training program should a parent worry that their child is not managing to go to the potty and get rid of diapers?

A. Generally, by the age of four most children are managing to use the potty successfully. There may be a problem if your toddler is not getting to the point of being potty trained by the age of four. A visit to your family doctor could help you understand if there is a problem to worry about.

#6. What do you do if you find your toddler is not happy with starting potty training?

A. There is no point in persisting with a reluctant toddler. Putting the process on hold for a while won't hurt and in the long run it is better to start the training when emotional readiness is reached as well as the physical and social stages.

#7. Why does it take longer for children to learn to poop on the potty?

A. Children may be fearful of the sensation of letting go of a bowel movement. It may take longer for this aspect of toileting to be under control. It is very important not to make issues with bowel movements. Recognize they happen and encourage using the potty or toilet. When accidents happen empty the poop into the potty and the into the toilet to show your toddler where poop goes and how to flush is away. Follow your routine with hand washing.

#8. What are the most popular words used for potty training?

A. Parents should choose these words carefully and try to use the words popular at play school or among families. You never know when your toddler may shout out their need for the bathroom. Using words commonly used for these functions makes it less embarrassing and easier for other people involved with your child to understand. The trend today is to raise children knowing the correct names for their body parts. However, the actual function of passing urine or having a bowel movement at a young age has its 'baby' name until children don't really talk about what they need to do. Urinating is usually called pee pee or wee wee. Boys generally seem to say pee and girls wee or some children say tinkle for needing to urinate. The poo or poo poo or doo doo and poop as well as doody are the most usual choice for a bowel movement. The overall action for going to the toilet can be 'go potty'. Generally, children outgrow these terms but while they are still learning it is easier to use terms used by most children and carers for these functions.

#9. How long does it take to train a toddler to use the potty?

A. There is no hard and fast time to mark off as the beginning and end of potty training. The thing to remember is your toddler is learning a new skill. It is a process and requires practice. It is not a race to reach the goal, the skill may take longer for different children. There may be ups and downs along the way but with patience and time your toddler will get the hang of using the potty or the toilet.

#10. Is it very difficult to toilet train your special needs child?

A. Depending on the measure of the disability you may need professional help. Here are some general tips to help in this area of expertise.

Potty training a special needs child

Potty training a special needs child will always be a different experience. Thankfully there are organizations, specialists, and support groups to help parents with their special needs children. Your toilet training routine will depend largely on the nature of your child's disability. It is very important when starting to train a special needs child to use the toilet or a potty that you take into consideration the developmental milestones and not their chronological age. Many of the readiness signs apply to a special needs child but the difference is a special needs children will have physical and mental delays.

Children with physical disabilities will have a problem with learning how to get on the potty or toilet. They may not be able to dress and undress themselves or wash their hands after using the toilet. There are very user-friendly toilet seats and training toilet facilities available for special needs children. It will take time and patience to work out what is best and most suitable for your special needs child.

Special needs children who are attending a facility or care center may learn how to use the potty or modified toilet for their use. Getting into a new routine can be difficult for children with developmental delays. Communication is an important factor. Nonverbal special needs children can learn signs to help with communication.

This process with special needs children will need an extra quota of patience and a calm reaction to accidents during the early stages of training. Rewards will help with communicating success. Try to watch your child's routine and find if there is a pattern you can work with. If you're struggling in any way don't be fearful of seeking professional help. There are many ways someone with experience in helping children with special needs will be able to help you find the successful route to toilet training.

ARE YOU MENTALLY PREPARED?

MENTAL PREPARATION:

Mental preparation may seem rather an intense part of potty training.

Many of us have heard of the expression of 'mind over matter." It is an expression linked to different philosophies and found in different contexts. Mind over matter is mind centered and linked to spiritual doctrine and psychology. It is the ability to put your mind over a physical condition and keep going. The theory has been cloned into a well-known phrase:

"Those who mind don't matter and those who matter don't mind!"

This could be a very consoling factor when, as a parent, you may find yourself struggling through the potty-training phase with your toddler. The mental preparation for this phase will help you to sort out what matters and what you don't need to mind about. Who matters in the process? Getting mentally prepared is very important.

There may be times when you feel close to war games, but by getting yourself into the right frame of mind your potty training could just go that much better. Have your strategy in place and make up your mind about how this training time is going to work for you and your toddler.

It doesn't have to be a war game, or a psychological thriller, as your toddler enters into a power struggle with you. Potty training done right is something of value and is actually the first step towards independence for your child.

George. S. Patton, American World War II general, and gifted tank commander, said:

> *"Better to fight for something,*
> *Than to live for nothing."*

How true is that for parents wanting to overcome the potty-training difficulties. Every parent wants to come out a winner with a well-trained child and a milestone for parenting accomplished.

Get ready in this chapter for some mind moves and preparation for the mental challenge of potty training.

And oh dear there is an accidental poop!

How will you react to an accident? This is a crucial question to ask. If you want to have a peaceful and productive potty-training experience be prepared for accidents Will you fly into a rage as you have just taken your toddler out of the bath and put on his pajamas and there is an accidental poop? Will you want to punish your child immediately? Will you feel totally anxious because your potty training is not working?

The answer is 'NO, rather be prepared' for accidents, they are bound to happen.

If you know things are not going to go perfectly the first time, or maybe not even the second or tenth time, then mentally you're prepared and being prepared is a big part of the battle. Tell yourself a little slip along the way is not the end of the journey. Sometimes it takes one step forward and two steps back before you really get going.

Here are some tips to make you feel pro-active and ready if an accident should happen.

- Have the potty in a convenient place easy to reach and ready for use.
- Put together a ready-made clean up kit for those little accidents. It could be a basket with some paper towel and a handy cleaning agent. Some rubber gloves for your protection and the necessary baby clean-up wipes with an emergency pair of pull ups or trainer pants. Keep all these items in a convenient place ready to grab if you need them in a hurry.
- Always take a nappy bag on outings with all the necessary

baby bits and pieces in case of an accident. Those handy bags to pop a dirty diaper or training pants into in case of an accident for disposal later. This makes an emergency situation less stressful.
- Keep some books or toys available as a distraction if you need some peaceful clean-up time.

Prevention is better than cure they say. How can you prevent an accident from happening? There may be signs you can look out for and words you can tell your child to use to signal they need the potty really quickly.

- Know your toddler well and look for signs that the potty may be needed. Signs like fidgeting or fiddling in the genital area signal a need to go to the potty.
- Teach your child a potty song to sing as a way of telling you they need the potty
- When you're at home make sure the bathroom door is always open for your toddler to gain easy access to the potty.
- Tell your child to head for the bathroom if they have an accident and call for your help. It is easier to clean up in the bathroom than on your new lounge carpet.

What kind of accidents can you expect?

- Once you start leaving your toddlers diaper free there is every chance, they will not make it to the potty in time and either wet the floor or poop in their trainer pants. It is a messy business, but also the beginning of awareness, as your toddler experiences passing urine or having a bowel movement.

- Little accidents in the cot at nap time can lead to big clean ups as your toddler decides to experiment with the mess created.
- Accidents when you're away from home or visiting grandma can be really upsetting. These are the occasions you need the travel bag of goodies for the accidental emergency.
- Accidents in the bath can cause drama if your toddler is sharing a bath with another sibling or if you have decided to have a quick bath together. Scooping up poop and heading for the toilet is not much fun, but you will feel glad that your toddler could be whisked out of the bath dried and dusted with powder and there's no harm done..

Know your temperament.

While you're preparing for potty training it may be useful to think about your temperament. Knowing the temperament type you're may help you understand how and why you react in certain ways. Are you naturally calm and controlled? Perhaps you're volatile and fly off the handle very easily. Think about your personality type and temperament. There are four basic types of temperament and sometimes a person may fall into two of the four categories. It is worth knowing these types of temperament and seeing how you fit into their areas.

The four types of temperament are:

1. **Sanguine**
2. **Phlegmatic**
3. **Melancholy**
4. **Choleric**

See if you fit any of these descriptions. Knowing your temperament may help you understand how you could react to potty-training time with your toddler. It is possible to have two temperament types overlapping each other and they would be known as primary and secondary types of temperament. Once you know the type of temperament you have you will be able to anticipate your reaction to accidents.

Sanguine:

This is the most common temperament type. This temperament type enjoys other people. They are out-going, talkative and like being sociable. Sanguine people don't mind working with other people. They are optimistic and entertaining. They build relationships with other people easily. They can be outspoken and hyperactive. Sometimes they are so busy enjoying themselves they forget what they are doing. They love sports and outdoor activities. Generally, they are fun to be with, but they do not like to be rejected and want to be accepted.

Phlegmatic:

This temperament is the other most common type, but is the opposite to sanguine. They tend to be introverted. They do work with others to reach a common goal. They are easy going and patient, but like to stick to a routine and are not so keen on making changes to this routine. Phlegmatic people like to live a quiet life. They are loyal family members. They are not quick decision makers and are seldom ambitious.

Melancholy:

This group sounds as if it is a depressed group with the use of the word melancholy. However, the word melancholy used here describes a cautious group of people. They are conscientious and like to find what is the right thing to do. Melancholy people can be perfectionists. They tend to be logical and analytical. This temperament is generally well organized, but can be anxious. They need all the information available before making a decision.

Choleric:

This temperament type is found less often in most people. Choleric people are extroverted and full of confidence. They are assertive and blunt in their communication style. They are risk takers, independent, and strong willed. This group of people are creative and always have good ideas, but they do not have many friends as they lack empathy with others.

Looking at these different character types may give you an idea of how you would cope with accidents in potty-training. In fact, knowing your character would help you with the whole process of potty training. You may be a combination of two of these traits. One being the primary character with the other being the secondary. None of these traits are perfect and each of them has elements of what might be seen as negative character in the face of potty training.

Sanguine:

Extrovert and outgoing, but so busy in their own world they forget the needs of others.

Phlegmatic:

Introverted, likes a routine, but doesn't like changes.

Melancholy:

Conscientious, but cautious. Organized, but anxious.

Choleric:

Extroverted full of confidence but lacking in empathy.

Identify the temperament that best suits your personality type and through knowing your personal pitfalls may help you overcome any emotional hang-ups that you could perceive as being part of your potty-training routine.

Now you have your own mind thinking right it is wise to remember your infant has a mind of their own too. Your baby's brain started developing way back when he or she was still wrapped up in your womb. The baby's brain doubles in size in the first year and by age three has reached 80% of its adult capacity. Dealing with a toddler up to the age of three means you're already dealing with a thinking, nearly fully wired, being. Toddlers are perfectly capable of playing mind games.

Starting to have a mind of their own is an important cognitive stage of development. This is part of exploring the world around them and they are sure to test your limits. Potty training is one of the key areas for these power struggles and your toddler soon recognizes it as the perfect time to push your boundary. The key to overcoming the power struggles associated with potty training, is to not overreact, and remember this is a training program. Acknowledge it will take time and you're teaching a skill. This is not about power it is about learning life lessons.

Here are three simple, but effective tips to help you stay calm during this time.

Tip # 1

<u>Be super organized</u> with everything you need and part of a routine you plan to have. Being organized and having everything gives you a sense of power over the situation. you're prepared. There may be some glitches, but overall, you have got this organized.

Tip # 2

<u>Make it fun</u> to take the pressure off both you and your child. Books, toys, songs, a rewards chart, choosing the right potty and neat clean undies all contribute to the positives of potty training. Try using a timer to sound out the next potty time. This gives your toddler a sense of control as they can call out – potty time! This can happen when the timer goes off. It gives them a small moment of being in control.

Tip # 3

<u>Be kind to yourself.</u> you're part of this team and during the time your toddler is potty-training don't forget to reward yourself in some way. When you're feeling strong and positive it is easier to be patient and consistent. You will feel the program is working.

Our words are powerful. We have the advantage over our toddlers because we have been speaking a lot longer than they have. Words can make or break a person's character. A crucial part of potty training is to use your words carefully. Build positive relationships as your child learns the skill of going to the toilet.

Success through potty training is a good time to boost your child and say positive phrases like:

> *'I am so proud of you.'*
> *'I know you did your best'*
> *'You make me feel happy'*
> *'I love being your mom/dad.'*
> *"You can try again tomorrow.'*
> *'You did that so well.'*

And so on – always encouraging and never angry or critical.

Avoiding some of the common mistakes made by parents and care givers at this time will help give you the peace of mind you may need as you and your toddler try to master this skill. Some of these suggestions may seem very obvious and some may make you think a little deeper about how to potty train successfully.

1. Never start to potty train when there are other stressful issues going on. Moving house, changing schools, welcoming a new baby into the home, family upsets or illness are all stressful and make learning something new difficult.
2. 'Don't make a big mountain out of an accident. Accidents happen. Deal with them on the occasion and then move onto something else.
3. Don't force your toddler to use the potty. It will not help if your child is not developmentally ready. Check all their developmental signs are noticeable and then start trying.
4. Don't let your toddler struggle with difficult clothing, be organized with comfortable clothes for your toddler that they can manage to pull on or take off. When you're at home let your toddler run around without a diaper on.
5. Don't dismiss any worries or doubts your toddler may have with regard to using the potty. Be sensitive to all the worries they may have about slipping off the seat if you're using a toilet seat, or the sound of the toilet flushing. Your toddler may have concerns about the stress of the poop they made being flushed away!

The best take away from being mentally prepared is best said in the three P's!

P patience, **P** perseverance and **P** plannin
...Three P's and excuse the pun.

P for patience, it is absolutely a key factor. You will have accidents, you will have days of being set back or your plan not going accordingly. You will need patience to get through this period. Patience will carry you a long way to success and is a big part of the mental process.

P for perseverance, keep going, you will get there in the end. Something will eventually stick in your child's mind and your patience will pay off. It definitely takes time, and you need to persevere.

P for planning, because it is important to plan and have a purpose, backed by the strategy you think will work best for our family and your child.

Mental preparation is just as important as the physical organization so do get yourself into the right mindset. Have your child onboard as well and together you will conquer the potty training process.

GETTING THE EQUIPMENT READY

EQUIPPING:

Preparation is the backbone of any event requiring some planning and organization. As parents know well, planning anything that involves young children, is guaranteed to need preparation. The first indication of this was getting ready for the birth of your baby. Suddenly it was a case of 'and baby makes three'. Life changes with the responsibility of an extra member in the family, especially as the new member is not able to decide or do much for themselves.

'By failing to prepare you're preparing to fail!'

— BENJAMIN FRANKLIN

Potty training, one of the most significant early childhood milestones, needs preparation. This is an event in your child's life that you want to succeed at. Every parent looks forward to the day diapers are ditched and their toddler becomes dry during the day. Then following on from daytime dryness comes the finale of blissful dry nights. Inevitably there are numerous commercial devices and recommended products available.

What do you choose as a parent? The first time round you want to do it right. Thereafter you're a bit more experienced, but may want to add to your potty training unit as new gadgets come on the market.

Here are some of the basics and some nice to have items in the potty department.

Potty, or potty chair, or toilet seat

The choice is really up to you and depends on the space you have in your bathroom and your toddler. Most parents like to-start out with a small potty. It is easy to store and can be moved from room to room if necessary. Potty chairs are more elaborate, and some can even flush. Take a trip to the baby department at the local store or a baby shop and see what is available. Whatever you choose you will need something for your child to sit on while they are learning about the toilet.

Bathroom step stool

You will need a step for your child to reach the taps and the wash basin. The step stool will also be needed for the step up to the toilet seat if you have decided on a toilet seat. It is important for the toddler in training to feel safe and secure. If your toddler is using different bathrooms have a step up for each bathroom so your toddler feels secure having the same equipment to use in each bathroom.

A faucet extender

The extender is another useful addition to the basin. The extender enables the child to engage with the water more easily as it comes into the basin via an extender. The extender may help to blend hot and cold together. If your water temperature in the hot tap is very hot, consider turning it down to a more moderate temperature while your child is learning to use the basin.

Underwear

Going out to choose big girl or big boy pants is a very exciting moment for your toddler. They will enjoy seeking out a superhero or favorite pretty panties for girls. You might prefer to start out with training pants with a more absorbent feel before venturing towards just undies. The important aspect of going from diaper to pants is your toddler can begin to feel what it is like to have wet or soiled underwear. Training pants are reusable and kinder on our planet.

Pull-ups

Pull ups can help your toddler to start out after a full-on diaper, but because they still absorb the urine, they do not give the experience of actually passing urine or having a bowel movement. Pull ups are a great help for nap times and nighttime or outings and traveling times.

There are more suggestions, for other reasons, to enhance your repertoire of gadgets. Training your toddler boy may be made easier with a potty and a splash guard. Transitioning from sitting to standing for little boys is made easier with some boy's specialties. Mini urinals for boys make learning to use a urinal easier for boys when they will need to know this for school and going to public toilets with dad.

Then if you're a traveler there is a range of toilet seats and portable potties you can fold up and off you go. Be prepared with your travel kit and a change mat, wet wipes, change of clothing, and the kind of trainer pants or pull ups you have decided to use.

There are so many different styles and purposeful potty-training types of equipment. Take some time to look at what is available on the internet and this will give you an idea of the different types of training support items and their prices. When you're familiar with what is on the market and you have the time to go potty shopping with your toddler you will have an idea of what you think is suitable and can afford.

Successful potty training will need some support material. One of the challenges initially is persuading your toddler to sit on the potty for a short space of time to get into the habit. Sitting and waiting for something to happen may not be in your toddler's understanding yet. Books are a great distraction.

Select some interesting books your toddler will enjoy looking at while you wait for the priceless sound of something finding its way into the potty. There are lovely potty books for children and potty stories to help get them in the mood. Add in some other intriguing books on subjects you know they are interested in. Pop-up and puzzle books help to engage your toddler in something that is going to hold their attention. Books will help your toddler sit in the right position to help them physically signal the brain it is time to do something in the potty. Repeating this habit of sitting, waiting, and looking at books could be the trigger that tells your toddler this is the time to go to the potty.

If you have the space in your bathroom set up a potty area with the potty or toilet seat ready for action. Include a basket of books and some toys your child enjoys playing with. Choose the kind of toys that keep your toddler happily engaged in doing something while they sit still. Stacking toys or shape posting toys for example. Playing music on a xylophone or even listening to potty songs and singing about the potty will be entertaining and keep your toddler suitably immobilized while you're there to help with the other toilet training routines.

Initially, when you first introduce the potty to your bathroom, bring in some toys and have some roleplay with the toys as they use the potty. A wetting doll, and there is a boy version, is a great help as your toddler can feed the doll and then watch as it wets in the potty. It is worth taking the time for some roleplay in the bathroom. Learning to wash hands and flush the toilet and become familiar with the toilet words will be helpful in the times to come.

The more time you take over the preparation, the more you're able to assess if your child is getting to the readiness phase of toilet training. If your toddler is not interested in anything you have to share about the toilet, and the routine, then you can be pretty sure they are not ready yet for toilet training. Try some other tactics to get their interest.

Here are some suggestions:

- Boys may enjoy dad or a big brother spending time with them talking about the boy's routine and how great it will be to go to the toilet like dad.
- Girls will enjoy a whole baby doll scenario with a changer and pampering corner for their wetting doll.
- Try some target practice for boys with the target gadgets you can put in the toilet
- Make up a toilet song you learn to sing together. The nursery rhyme 'Here we go round the Mulberry bush' is very adaptable and easily adds onto the list of things to do round the mulberry bush. The rhyme already has a verse for washing hands. Take the liberty of adding on other activities that are part of your toilet routine.

Rewards

The debate about rewards for potty training is ongoing.

There is really no right or wrong answer about rewards. Think about why you're giving a reward and how you plan to celebrate with the reward incentive. Sometimes a little incentive goes a long way towards encouraging success. The danger is over doing the hype around rewards and ending up with a fearful child who is not able to perform and please you. The other danger is a power struggle as your toddler realizes going to the potty is REALLY important to you! These are some of the debatable questions parents ask about rewards.

Q. Should you reward your toddler for a basic life skill?

A. Responsible parents don't want to fall into the trap of rewarding every little thing their child does. Developing a routine at home for day-to-day activities like brushing teeth and brushing hair soon lets them know there are some things we all do just because they are part of our lives. When we get out of bed in the morning we are not rewarded. A little incentive to kick start learning a new skill is not a bad idea. Using the potty correctly and reading your body signs is a new skill. The difficulty is keeping the rewards and the hype about the milestones reached at a realistic level. All things in moderation so rewards do not get out of hand.

Q. Can too much hype around rewards lead to power struggles between you and your toddler?

A. Yes, your toddler is smart and quick to pick up on the things that make you happy and sad. Manipulation is a great weapon, and a smart toddler will soon pick up on the body language and reactions you have towards potty training. This is where your patience will be tested. The moment you see the signs of your child trying to wield power over you, stop and take a rain check on your potty-training. You will soon know if trying to get positive results out of potty-training is becoming a power struggle. Then it is time to back away and leave the potty story till a bit later.

Q. Does a reward system cause too much stress if your toddler is unable to perform and therefore, unable to get a reward?

A. Yes, the stress of trying to perform on demand will upset your child especially if they are not ready for potty training. Look back on the signs that your child is ready. Keep a careful watch on your child's routine bowel movements and when they may want to urinate. These signs will help you understand if there is a routine time you can tap into. Just take it all one step and one day at a time because your child may not be ready yet.

Q. What are the best rewards, something tangible or intangible?

A. Tangible rewards, like prizes or sweeties, need to be monitored carefully. There are different ideas for these rewards. The tangible rewards can become close to bribes. Have a plan or rewards chart to help with the way they are given and are not just an expected reward.

Intangible rewards of words of affirmation and applause or high fives and giant claps are great ways to reward without the expectation of a gift or a sweet. There is also a danger of over doing the physical hype of the reward and putting too much pressure on your child to perform. They will feel worried that without something in the potty, you're going to be disappointed, and the song and dance will not happen.

Q. Do you reward for every little thing or do you modify the rewards?

A. The best approach is to keep it simple and look at the age of your toddler too. If they are ready for a rewards chart this is a great way to build up to a success level and offer a reward for reaching a target. In this way there is evidence of goal setting and an incentive to try harder to reach the goal. Together you can calculate at the end of the week how many stickers have been won. You do want to encourage your child to have a sense of pride in what they do and not to have their hands out for a reward for everything they do around the house.

Now you have your set up ready. Find time for roleplay in the bathroom as you show your toddler how everything functions. If you have older siblings, they will be very eager to show a younger brother or sister how the bathroom works. Make plenty of time to talk about this new skill. It is a big deal however you look at it. A big step towards independence and finding control over a bodily function for your toddler. It is a big milestone for you as your toddler progresses towards independence.

Try not to take learning to use the potty for granted. It is not like learning to sit or walk. Give them time and space and some rewards for encouragement.

Dr Seuss has a great way of putting adult philosophies into childlike context. Next time you're feeling frustrated about potty training take heed of these words.

"I'm glad we had the times together just to laugh and sing a song,
Seems like we just got started and then before you know it,
The times we had together were gone."

Potty training, and the preparation for the event, is just a short time in your child's life. It is an important part of the time you will share with your child.

THE 7 STEP PLAN FOR POTTY TRAINING YOUR CHILD IN JUST A FEW DAYS

Well done! You're ready for the 7-step plan!

You've completed the TIME section.

Let's take a look at the POTTY part and get into the practical side.

The show must go on! Right? you're prepared, equipped and ready to start.

In the days of the circus arena the ringmaster would always say -

'The show must go on!'

Regardless of a missing elephant or a trapeze artist without a trapeze, the show would and did go on. Now it is time for your potty show to go on. You have rehearsed, you know your lines and the stage is set.

The star is waiting in the wings. Costumes and props are ready. The program is ready to follow. It's time to check the seven-step plan has been accomplished and the show is ready to rock and roll, it's the opening moment for potty time.

Let the show begin!

Go through the seven steps to be ready to pull back the curtains and let the star step into the limelight.

Step #1. Rehearsals

Have you had some rehearsals to prepare for the event? Taking time to practice using the potty is a very strategic part of the seven steps. You could have had some roleplay with toys or with yourself as you spent time in the bathroom setting everything out in the potty area. Reading books about the potty is another way to rehearse the event.

Step # 2. Know your lines

This is the step where you have taught your child the words you plan to use for going to the toilet and for what is done there. Try to choose words used by their playschool if your child is going to a preschool. Make sure your child can follow simple instructions like wash hands or flush the toilet. Does your child know how to ask you for the toilet or how to help with the wiping process? These are all part of the lines you may want to teach. Check they know the words for the toiletries and how to get your attention and avoid an accident.

Step #3. Set the stage

At this step you need to check you have set up the area in the bathroom with all the toilet equipment you will need. You have chosen wisely from the range of potties, potty chairs or toilet seats. Include in this any extras you may think your child will enjoy to make this event manageable. Your child needs to know how to make an entrance to the stage and how to exit.

Step #4 The star is ready

You have checked and the star is ready for this experience. The star knows the lines, the way to use the stage and what it means to start using the potty. The star is well rehearsed and ready to perform.

Step #5 The program

The program for the show is planned and everyone knows their part. There is an opening time and a closing time. Time for breaks and time for each act to take place. The stage is set. When the curtains open, and the show begins, everyone will be ready for this great moment.

Step #6 costume and props

The right clothing is ready. You have decided on training pants or undies. Pull ups are available if you need them for an emergency or for your initial nighttime sessions. You have added in some books and a faucet gadget if you think one will make a difference. You have some planned distractions and games to play if you need your toddler to focus and spend more time in the bathroom.

Step #7 Applause, applause and Oscars to be awarded

Hooray your potty star has performed with success and everyone gets a standing ovation for their performance. This is the time to bring out your rewards and congratulate your child on the part they played. you're hoping for encores and a repeat performance.

Those are your seven steps to success. Go through them again and tick them off in your head and decide if your child is good and ready for the real thing. If in doubt perhaps you need some more rehearsal time before you launch into your show.

When you're ready for the show to go on it may only take a weekend to finish off the training you have been doing.

The three day weekend method is available to you to try when you're confident you have covered the seven step plan to being ready. The three day plan requires all your time and attention for the three days. It is recommended, especially if you're a working parent or life during the week is too hectic with other siblings, that you take a day off from work or from the family and be ready to spend three days of intense training time with your toddler. This plan is going to be all about being committed to using the potty throughout the day. Parents or the designated trainer for the three days must be 100% focused on the task.

Part of the prep will be to tell your toddler what to expect for the three day potty extravaganza. You remove the last diaper on the morning that you begin your potty training in the three-day potty-training approach. You tell your toddler that is the end of diapers.

Be prepared for accidents. The three-day potty-training method recommends that for success your child should go bottomless. Use some old extra-long t-shirts to cover the child's private area, but have no diaper or trainers underneath. You want your toddler to feel what happens when they pass urine or have a bowel movement. Some parents opt for training pants or undies, but remember the point of the exercise is for your toddler to learn about their bodily functions. You will be on hand to explain what is happening or to help your toddler to the potty.

There needs to be a rigorous time schedule and lots of liquid input because you want their bladder to work. Throughout the day you will take your toddler to the bathroom to use the potty. Every 30 minutes is a good interval for this, but watch for the signs from your toddler and try not to build up resistance before you have started. Sometimes you may be lucky sometimes not. The 30-minute intervals is just for the 3 day training session there after children should go at strategic times like on waking, before and after breakfast, before and after snack time and lunch time and before and after nap time and last thing before bed. Getting into this routine will help your child's bodily functions fit into a rhythm too.

At the end of the three days, you will be the judge based on your toddler's performance. How did it go in the end? Ask yourself if your toddler was conscientious about telling you or showing you their efforts. Did you feel there was a real awareness of what it means to use the potty and the bathroom? If so, then you're on the right track and you should see a difference in your child's ability to get to the toilet or call you for help. If you did not notice a difference, then your toddler was not ready for this step. It would be best for everyone to go back to diapers and perhaps use training pants when your child is out in the garden. There is no harm done if you just go back to the beginning again and start your steps over again another time.

Leave all the preparation in place. Your toddler may just say out of the blue one day that they want to use the potty. Try again when you're ready, but do not force the issue of using the potty. The training tactics you choose are really the one that fits best with your home life and the temperament of your child. Read up on all the different methods and then try the one that you think gives you the most confidence that it could work.

Here are three other methods you could try

The Child Orientated (CO) or the Brazelton approach

This method depends entirely on the child being interested as the parent takes them through four different steps.

- Step one: Getting to know the potty and sitting on it fully dressed. The message is - yay the potty is fun.
- Step two: Sit on the potty without pants or a diaper, some praise, but not too much. It's still just fun.
- Step three: Sit on the potty after soiling a diaper. The contents of the diaper are put in the potty. The toddler is told this is where poop and pee go. They go in the potty and then into the toilet.
- Step four: The child goes without a diaper for a short while and is encouraged to sit on the potty. They may use the potty

and that is celebrated as a success. If they do not use the potty the system is put on hold and the CO process may start again sometime later. It is a slow process, but eventually the toddler reaches the point when using the potty comes naturally.

- DIY: The entire process is left to the toddler to sort out physically and mentally. All the right equipment is provided, and your toddler gets to figure it out by spending some time outside with no undies on and knowing the potty is there for their use when the time is right for them. This method relies on peer pressure and imitating family members. There is absolutely no pressure, but it can take a really long time.
- Parent-led potty training: Parents draw up a schedule of potty visits and lead their child to the potty at those particular times. The times fit in with meals and naps and bedtime and times in between. The schedule takes into account the observations of times when the toddler did wee or poop and tries to factor those times in between. This method relies on a parent or caregiver to be there all the time to help the child who is learning.

Added to these is the three day method. The three day method is more demanding on parents and has the added messy component. It may not suit everyone. However, of all the methods out there, the three day method has the highest success rate ratio in the proportion to the shortest time. It does rely heavily on your child being ready for this method and potty training as a whole.

Taking a break.

The idea of taking a break is definitely one to consider. It helps to put some time and space between the pressure of getting the training right and having a good relationship with your toddler. Taking a break is not a sign of failure. It is just giving yourself and your toddler some breathing space and time to regroup. You will get it right, you're just taking a break, having a rain check or some time out. An interval.

What are some of the reasons why you would take a break?

Ever you heard the following expression?...

> 'You can take a horse to water, but you can't make it drink!'

If potty training makes you feel like that then it is time to take a break. The more you try to force the issue the more stubborn and difficult your toddler may get.

Here are some other common reasons for taking a break:

- Refusal to sit on the potty. Don't force it your child is not ready.
- Not able to pull pants on and off. This may cause frustration and a bad attitude to going to the potty.
- Your toddler is not ready to follow simple instructions. Not ready for toilet training, still too dependent on you.
- you're still trying to find a pattern to your toddler's bowel movements.

- Your toddler is just not able to sit still for long enough to stay on the potty.
- Feelings of fear from your toddler to sit on the potty or the toilet seat.
- Something happening at home that is a disruption to routine or a disturbance to the family life. Like moving or expecting another baby.

Whatever reasons come your way just take the break and regroup. Come back to potty training and you will be glad you did take some time out.

When you return to try again you may find your toddler has matured and is ready to try again. This time round you may be able to get the process done in record time and the transition from diaper to big boy/girl pants will be very easy. Potty training will never happen in less than a week if your toddler is not ready. You may have done everything in your power to get there, but it is never going to be possible if your toddler is not ready.

Readiness is defined as a stage when a child is able to learn easily without emotional constraints. The emotional readiness may not be something parents see easily, but it is there, and emotional outbursts are very typical of the two- and three-year-old. In order for a child to reach the emotional readiness other experiences will be contributing to this state of readiness. The potty experiences, the stories and the games, the role play and the potty toys and the rewards and encouragement. You will find after a break the readiness is there and you can start again.

The ultimate aim is to ditch the diaper. It will be the greatest feeling of freedom!

This is what ditching the diaper will mean to you, your family and the planet. Ditching diapers means:

- No more allergies and rashes for your toddler.
- You will save money on no longer buying such expensive commodities.
- Potty training and using the toilet becomes easier.
- Going on outings is quicker and you can organize yourself with less baggage.
- Playschools prefer children to be potty trained without diapers.
- Ditching diapers means freedom for your child. Freedom to run, climb, explore, and move around without a cumbersome diaper between their legs.
- Ditching the diaper is the first big milestone in your child's road to independence.
- It is the first sign of gaining control over their own bodily functions.
- Ditching diapers has a positive impact on our planet as the number of disposables dumped in landfills every day is astronomical. It is estimated that 3.5 billion dirty diapers are dumped in landfills per year.
- To ditch diapers sooner will make a small contribution to changing these horrific statistics.

When you're confident that you have followed the steps and chosen your training method or training style. When you have found the calm and patient spirit within you to master the process of potty training your child, you will be ready to experience success and to tick the box that says you did it, you managed to potty train your toddler and see them dry through the day.

Bask in the sunshine of this achievement before tackling the night-time routine.

13

WHAT TO DO AT NIGHTTIME WHEN TOILET TIME ARISES...

OVERNIGHT, AND NO UNNECESSARY BAGGAGE:

Nighttime should, and can be, the time in your toddler's routine you're looking forward to. The end of the day when you wind down together and go through a bedtime ritual, finishing with a sleeping, angelic child wrapped up in bed. This is the ideal situation, and you may be getting close to that, but now there is another potty milestone ahead of you and that is nighttime training!

Here is the good news. Nighttime potty training is not the same as daytime training. The ability to stay dry at night is very dependent on your child's physiological development and the readiness of the brain and bladder's neural pathways, connecting the right neurons to send signals from one part of the brain to another. There are signs to watch out for and things to do to prepare for nighttime training, but the whole experience will be different compared to your daytime training. In other words, it is like day and night – different in many ways. Keeping developmental milestones in mind will make it easier to feel less stress as you lead up to nighttime potty training.

Nighttime readiness comes much later in your child's developmental milestones. Remember each child is different and their readiness for nighttime training will be different from other children.

These are average age developmental signs to watch for as you observe your child's readiness to start nighttime training.

- **Age 1** – you will notice there is less poo-ing in the night.
- **Age 2** – at this early stage your toddler may be dry during the day.
- **Age 3** – 9/10 children are dry during the day.
- **Age 4** – Most children are dry during the day.
- **Age 5** – 85% - 90% of children are able to stay dry at night.

The exceptions may have medical reasons for their delay.

Nighttime training is not recommended until daytime training is completed.

Here are the other signs to look for to decide on your appointment time with night training. Take some time to reflect on your vision for this night training. Night training does not have to be a burden. You may find it easier than daytime training.

Carl Jung, a well-known psychoanalyst said this about vision:

> *"Your vision will become clear when you look into your own heart.*
> *He who looks outside dreams, He who looks inside awakens."*

You do not have to have this deep sense of dread that you will be dealing with sleepless nights as you try to potty train at all hours of the night. There are signs to look for and preparation, then you let nature take its course and without too much stress the nighttime potty monster will have been dealt with.

Signs and tips to remember:

Dry during the day

This is most important. If you have not successfully managed the day routine, making allowance for the odd accident, then your toddler is not ready for the nighttime potty training.

Check family history

Were there any bed wetters in the family?

This is valuable information. Bed wetting or incontinence at night as a young child can follow in the family history. Medically this is known as nocturnal enuresis. It is the unintentional passing of urine during the night.

Can your toddler manage pull-ups if they want to use the potty in the night?

You may want to put out the nighttime potty and explain to your toddler there is a potty to use in their room if they want to go during the night. It will help if your child can manage to pull down the nighttime pull ups you have transitioned into.

Is your toddler in a bed without cot sides yet?

Your toddler needs to be able to get out of bed to get to the potty. Most toddlers have moved out of their cots at this stage.

Are you finding dry diapers in the morning?

As soon as your child wakes and gets out of bed try to get there and check if the diaper or pull-ups were dry through the night. Then run off to the potty so their bladder can work bright and early.

Can your child run off to the bathroom as soon as they awake?

Training your toddler to take themselves to the potty first thing when they wake is a very good habit. Then you will be able to check for a dry diaper from the night before.

Can your toddler do without too much fluid in the evening?

Less fluids after supper makes a difference to the amount of water the bladder can hold onto during the night.

Are you prepared for the nighttime routine?

You may have your bedtime routine sorted, but you need to be ready for anything that could go wrong during the night. There is nothing worse than scrabbling around at night with a crying wet baby. Rather get prepared for the nighttime. This is the time between going to sleep after your bedtime ritual and waking early in the morning.

Preparation for Nighttime potty training

Part 1 - The bedtime routine

First thing to check is have you sorted your bedtime routine and is your toddler used to this routine? It should include the following components. Adjust it according to your family needs.

The bedtime routine actually starts a while before bedtime with ending off the afternoon activities. A tidy up time and then a nice warm bath. Soaking in the warm water and playing with a few bath toys is a perfect way to unwind your toddler. Depending on your toddler's age have a family supper or feed your toddler earlier. Family suppers are good bonding times so take advantage of that. Start to warn your toddler of bedtime coming up. Keep everyone calm because any hype will trip your toddlers calm switch and you will get a little one high wired and not ready for bed.

Limit drinks at this time. If your toddler is still having a comfort bottle at bedtime, then they are not ready to potty train. The immature bladder is not able to hold too much water at this stage. Your toddler may be a deep sleeper and not feel the warning signs from the bladder to say it is full. Take your toddler for a quick potty time about thirty minutes before bed then you take then again right before bed. This is like a double dose of trying out the potty.

The last, but not quite least element of the bedtime routine, is the bedtime story. One or two or more stories, it is entirely up to you! There needs to be an ending time, or a limit on the number of stories, or you're going to open yourself to some manipulation.

The story time really helps to calm down your toddler at the end of the day. It is a good time for some language development and incidental learning about the world. Use the time to your best advantage. When story time is over put the books away and visit the potty again for one last time before turning out the main lights. A night light will be comforting if your toddler needs to get up to use the potty.

Then its night-night,

Don't let the bugs bite,

See you in the morning light.

The time it takes for your toddler to fall asleep will depend on their activity level during the day and their own personalities helping them unwind and fall asleep. During the night they may be heavy or light sleepers, but you will want to be prepared for the night run. Preparation for the night is part two of getting ready for nighttime training.

Part 2 - preparation for the nighttime

There are a few things to purchase to ease into your nighttime training.

- A waterproof mattress or waterproof fitted cover to protect your toddler's mattress.
- Easy pull on and off pajamas or night clothes.
- Readily available spare bedding and a spare blanket.
- Easy access to the potty or potty chair at night.
- A night light.
- Pull ups rather than a diaper because they are easier to pull up or down at night.

This is a helpful suggestion for the night emergency. Try to stop fumbling and getting frustrated in the middle of the night. Initially set yourself up with a double set of bedding. Lay one set of sheets and plastic protector on top of another on your toddler's bed. If you have a nighttime accident you simply remove the top set of wet bedding and voila there is a bottom set ready and waiting.

Be prepared to be patient.

Patience will once again be needed to conquer nighttime potty training. Remember you're expecting your toddler to form a new habit. The new behavior of getting out of bed when nature calls to go to the toilet or potty. All this mental activity and convincing of the brain can only take place when the brain has reached that state of physiological development. It is common belief that it takes 21 days to form a new habit, but it could take 66 days. Neuroscientists claim that it is quicker to start a new habit than stop an old one. That is encouraging for parents of toddlers, because they are breaking new ground all the time. The point is learning to go to the potty at night is trying to form a new habit and takes time and patience.

Being able to use the potty or toilet at night is a vital life skill and because it is dependent on being ready and willing it will take different children different lengths of time to grasp the habit. This is a developmental step that is not age related, but links directly with developmental milestones. In addition, the process could be slowed by a child who is a heavy sleeper and does not wake easily to go to the potty. Some parents like to wake their toddler and sit them on the potty half sleep to see if they can perform before the parents go to bed. This is a personal choice and perhaps you should try it and see if your very heavy sleeper just goes right off back to sleep and remains dry for the night. Or you run the risk of waking your toddler who now thinks it is time to get up and go while you're ready for bed.

An old Irish proverb says:

'A good laugh and a long sleep are the best cures in the doctor's book.'

Hopefully you will look back on potty training with a few laughs and generally get a good night's sleep too.

Finding your child has regressed is never a laughing matter. It happens though. There could be a number of reasons for regression.

Stress is usually one of the foremost reasons for potty training setbacks. If you find your toddler, who was keeping quite dry in the day, is having some regressive moments don't worry. This is quite normal and usually temporary. It could be as simple as being engrossed in a play activity and leaving a trip to the toilet too late. If you experience a setback look into your family circumstances at that time. Perhaps there is a root cause for a setback or regression often caused by stress.

Here are some common stress factors.

- Moving house.
- Expecting another sibling.
- Changing schools.
- An accident at home or at school.
- A family trauma or loss.
- Illness.

In fact, any number of out of the ordinary events can trigger a stress factor. Parents need to be sympathetic and recognize a few days of regression are not going to stop their toddler moving forward again when the time is right. It is easier to accept it is a momentary set back. When the stress is over things will get back on track.

Other more serious factors could cause a regression, and these may need medical attention or some extra support at that time from the family or the caregivers.

Take your child for a medical checkup if you suspect an underlying issue like constipation or a urinary tract infection. Refusal to use the potty could be linked to feeling overly tired or out of the normal routine.

Parents could be at the root of the problem if there is too much pressure on a toddler to perform when they are not really ready. Added to the emotional pressure to use the potty could be your toddler's inability to tell you what they need at the time. These acts of perceived regression probably go back to the issue of readiness.

The best advice is not to see this as regression. It is just a temporary recess.

What should you do at this time?

- Be supportive.
- Do not punish your child, but try to find the root cause.
- Discuss the problem with the school or with a medical practitioner.
- Go back to basics again.
- Add some incentives and a rewards chart to get back on track.
- Bring out the favorite potty books or buy a new funny one to laugh at together.
- Spend more time with your toddler especially if there is a new sibling in the family. Try reassuring your toddler and deal with any anxiety they may be feeling towards this new person in your family.
- Increase confidence and self-esteem. Do something fun together and explain this is for big boys and girls who are not babies in diapers any longer.

The most important factor is not to despair, this is quite common during potty training. You may feel this is regression, but you will regain the ground you think you have lost, and the little delay will not matter when you see the bigger picture.

The bigger forward vision of a toddler free of diapers and ready to run ahead conquering other milestones in their early years.

Getting Help from Daycares and Caregivers

TODDLER CARERS:

It is time for teamwork.

> **"Individual commitment – to a groups effort is what makes a team work."**

14

GETTING HELP FROM DAYCARES AND CAREGIVERS

TODDLER CARERS:

I t is time for teamwork.

"Individual commitment – to a groups effort is what makes a team work."

— VINCE LOMBARD

Although Vince Lombard was an acclaimed American Football coach, his words are relevant to choosing a successful daycare organization or a caregiver. You want to work together for the common goal of the health and well-being of your child.

Before choosing your team, you need to do some research and understand exactly what it is you're looking for. Here are some points to ponder on.

- What are your needs, and most importantly, what are your child's needs?
- What different kinds of facilities are available in your area?
- Do you want your child to stay at home or in a home environment?
- Would you prefer a registered care institution with all the extra facilities offered by an organization?
- Do you need full day care or part-time care?
- What phase of your child's development are you wanting care for? Infant, toddler or preschool?
- Can you find the right facility close to you or on your route to work?
- Are you just looking for some mental stimulation and socializing for your child?

These are all considerations to make while you're searching for the right facility. The facility may have different names, but the services offered are similar. A daycare center, a day nursery, a nursery school and a creche (French for crib) are all the same type of facility. They offer degrees of care for young children from babies or infants to preschool. Looking for one of these facilities would mean you're preparing to register your child at a center away from home.

Perhaps you would rather have your child stay comfortably in your own home or in a home environment. In this case you would be looking for a caregiver. A qualified person who would come into your home and care for your child while you're at work. You may know someone who has a care facility in their own home with a limited number of children. You may be prefer to have a family member, perhaps a grandparent, who would be the caregiver.

All these options have their own sets of criteria to consider. They may be privately owned or attached to your workplace but in the interests of children there are regulations and standards to adhere to. The need for facilities for children while women go back to work has become more prevalent in this century. In 2001 it was recorded that 64% of mothers with children under 6 years old were going back to work and 78% of mothers with children age between 6 and 17 were fully employed in the workplace.

What does a center-based daycare offer that parents can depend on? These are questions to ask to find out if this kind of facility will support your overall mantra of:

'Individual commitment to a group effort to make a team work.'

What do care centers offer?

- They are facilities offering care for groups of children.
- They may be attached or sponsored by an educational

institution, a church, a social welfare organization, or privately owned.

- They should follow standards set by communities and child welfare organizations.
- They should follow regulations to cover staff ratio to children, children and the space allocated to them, ablution facilities, and follow any other health and safety regulations.
- The facility should have qualified staff trained with experience in your child's age group and learning developmental areas.
- A day care center will always be able to provide facilities because it is not dependent on one person, there is a team of people, the staff.
- There will be interaction with other children at the care center and opportunities to develop social skills.
- Cognitive and creative development is included in the program.
- A registered day care should have more outdoor and indoor equipment for the children. There should be adequate indoor and outdoor space to interact.

<u>There may be some disadvantages to a daycare center to consider in your decision.</u>

- A day care center may be costly. Weigh up the advantages of being part of an organized facility cost wise compared with the other options.

- Staff turnover may be higher and unsettling for children who form a bond with a particular care giver at the facility.
- Larger groups of children will mean less individual attention. The individual attention could be something parents would want for very young children.
- There is greater exposure at a day care center to infections and contagious diseases. Young children have to build up their immunity to these infections.

Family care provider.

A family care provider may not necessarily be a member of your family. This form of care is a trained person who is offering a care facility in their home, with a small group of children. This kind of facility has regulations to fulfill and should be registered with your local authority. There are guidelines for the children's protection and safety. The facility should be inspected to check on the regulations and the caregiver should have a criminal background check.

There are advantages to this facility.

- It would be especially suited to very young children who may be unable to cope with a large care center.
- The ratio of child to carer is much smaller and children will get more individual attention.
- Smaller groups may find it easier to socialize initially.
- The home carer will get to know your child well and be able to form a close bond.

There are some disadvantages to consider if you're thinking of using a home facility.

- A family carer in their own home may not have as much equipment as a registered day care center.
- The family carer may not be registered and that needs to be checked.
- There is a risk if only one person is running the facility that there is no backup should that person fall ill.
- The facility is dependent on one person for the activities and stimulation offered with a home-based caregiver.

Finally, there is personal help with a carer coming to your home.

You may want your child to stay at home with a care giver or a registered nanny for the early stages of development if you have to go back to work. You may need a carer to help if you work from home. Your type of work needs you to have some time and structure to enable you to continue with your work schedule. A nanny or Au pair would suit you with a very young child.

How does this kind of care facility work and what are the advantages?

- It would be best to go through an agency because they will have done all the security and criminal record checks required.
- You can interview the incoming nanny to see if she is a good fit for your family.

- You will have control over what happens with regard to the care of your child.
- Your child will feel safe in the confines of their own home.
- Care will be available even if your child is not well.
- You may have a live in carer and have the advantage of extra help whenever you need it.

There are some disadvantages to consider.

- This is an expensive option because of the cost of an individual carer.
- When your child is ready to develop social skills there will not be other children in the mix unless you organize play dates and interaction with other children.
- The equipment you offer is dependent on the facilities you have at home.

<u>You may consider care from a family member, relative, or close friend.</u>

This is often a very convenient option and may not cost too much. It really depends on your relationship with the family and friends. Will this offer the teamwork you're looking for? Consider the convenience against the added facilities of somewhere that is organized for childcare.

There are advantages to what is affectionately known as 'Kith and Kin care'

- More loving and personal care as a family member is involved.
- You will share common values and beliefs because the person is part of your extended family.
- There may be more flexibility with using a relative or family member.
- Little or no cost incurred.

The disadvantages would be the ones you weigh up as you assess your personal relationship with the family carer and what they are capable of offering.

How does the teamwork mantra fit over all these different options?

Ask yourself if the facility or service you choose offers that special individual commitment to your child. Will the type of care you organize be giving that extra special commitment to your child and form part of the team that has a unified goal to give the best care to young children?

If you're contemplating care facilities for your child here are some guidelines to consider or questions to ask yourself before you start your search.

- Convenience and availability.
- Operating hours.
- Additional after care hours of facilities should you need them.
- Part time or flexibility hours.
- Costs, is it affordable for your budget.

- Quality of staff their qualifications.
- Staff child ratio.
- Curriculum.
- Equipment indoor and outdoor.
- Potty training.
- Safety regulations.
- Policy for sick children.
- Parenting style of the facility.
- Schedule.
- Schedule for sleep times and feeding times.
- Provision of food.
- Discipline policy.
- Communication with parents.
- Open door policy.
- Are parents encouraged to visit?

How do you check facilities?

The best way is to set up an appointment to visit the facility. Book an appointment time to meet the supervisor or head of the care center and request a tour of all the classrooms, not just the one your child will be part of. This gives you a chance to see how your child will progress through the facility and if there is a program in place for creativity and cognitive growth. Look at the outdoor facilities. Do they provide the kind of climbing and physical activities you're seeking for your child? Ask about creative activities and how children's creativity and sensory development is catered for. Ask about the routine and any other questions you feel you want to know about on a day-to-day basis.

Word of mouth is another good way to check a facility. Listen to what other parents have to say about the facility in your area. However, always do your own physical check too. You may be lucky and have a daycare section attached to the primary school or to your workplace.

Whatever our options are always see for yourself if this is the best for your child's needs and the right amount of care you're looking for.

What should you look for in caregivers?

- Knowledge of child development.
- Qualifications in the area of child education.
- Physical fitness.
- Creativity.
- Interpersonal skills.
- Command of language to be able to communicate and send reports of child progress.
- First aid certificate.

Teamwork with potty training.

Top three important goals.

One: Follow a common routine initially.
Two: Use the same potty and toilet training words to ease the process of asking for and using the potty or toilet.
Three: Give rewards and praise for encouragement linking what is achieved at school with what goes on at home to boost morale and acknowledge success.

Expectations from your daycare and child caregivers.

The expectations of your chosen daycare should be higher because there will be more trained personnel and equipment available. The curriculum and structure should offer more classes and therefore, further facilities for your child as they go through the daycare program. The daycare program should cover the full range of ages they advertise they cater for. Some care facilities may only offer a specific age range others may go all the way from infant to the school readiness stage. It all depends on what you're looking for in terms of the admission age for your child.

Each daycare institution should be aiming to cover the following developmental areas at the appropriate level of understanding. There should be a curriculum that is being followed based on these areas and the age-appropriate developmental milestones.

- Cognitive development.
- Physical development.
- Gross and fine motor skills.
- Social skills.
- Language and communication.
- Creativity.
- Emotional development.
- Life skills.

When to consult a specialist?

The advantage of having your child at a daycare center or with a qualified caregiver is you will have insight into their development from an early age. The earlier you get help for any of your child's problems the better for their healthy growth and happiness. While your child is with a care center they will be observed. You should receive regular reports and the caregiver or daycare center will be watching the milestones that the average child should reach.

These are the areas your caregivers and daycare centers should be monitoring.

- Physical age-appropriate developmental milestones.
- Emotional development.
- Social skills.
- Language Development.
- Cognitive developmental.
- Interpersonal skills with teachers and other children.
- Maturity.
- Gross and fine motor skills.
- Ability to listen and concentrate.

All of these areas are measurable against standardized norms. Children do develop at different rates and have different strengths and weaknesses. However, when there is a norm to compare with and the caregiver or center is concerned this is a good opportunity to get advice and see a specialist.

The delays may simply be a normal pattern of development and your child will catch up. The delay or difficulties could be for other reasons and a pediatrician or child psychologist could help discover the problem and refer your child for some further intervention. There is such a range of possible interventions from an auditory processing problem to something more serious. Finding the root cause to any delays or difficulties your child may have before they reach primary school will make all the difference to your child's self-esteem, confidence, and academic progress.

When you consider all the help and advice available for raising healthy happy children it is easy to see why a team approach is a positive way forward.

Henry Ford, the creator of the original assembly line for car manufacturing, said:

"If everyone is moving forward, success takes care of itself."

Try to see hiring a care giver or registering your child at a daycare center as a way of moving forward with your child. They are the professional and you chose them carefully. This time in your child's life should contribute to their moving forward experience as you and anyone involved with the progress of your child moves forward.

RAISING THE HAPPIEST CHILD AROUND

TOTALLY UNDERSTANDING

How to raise the happiest Kid around.

You may, or may not, be surprised to read material things do not make children the happiest kid around. Fleeting moments of happiness experienced perhaps for a sweet treat or a bigger spoiling like a toy or a game, but these tokens of happiness are not lasting and do not make for long term or genuinely happy children.

Real happiness comes from within. It is about being nurtured and being loved. Children need a sense of security, a feeling of belonging to something greater than themselves. They need food and shelter and positive optimistic feelings around them.

Here is a check list of things to remember to encourage and motivate towards being a happy, well balanced child.

Provide nurturing

Think about what it means to nurture. It is not just about feeding and clothing. Nurture embraces the concept of caring in every way to help a person develop, grow, and succeed. Nurturing assists a child to get to the point where they are using their talents in the best way possible.

Nurture yourself too

Remember you need to look after yourself during this time. If you feel broken and weak you will not be able to nurture, raise, and care for your children.

Believe in the mantra of, hard work and practice

This is the way to achieve goals. There is so much truth in this small statement. Keep it close to your heart.

Notice success and failure

Help your child to see if you failed you're not a failure. Speak openly about failure to succeed and how your child can see success and failure as achievements. We learn from our mistakes.

Praise is important

Praise is a wonderful way to encourage and uphold children for their contribution. Try to give out praise with encouraging comments for different achievements not just academics or sporting success.

Compliment effort made not just success

Sometimes effort and focus are the outcome of an endeavour. Parents who can praise the effort made are helping their children to feel appreciated.

Teach your child to be optimistic

Being optimistic goes a long way to being happy. Look at the glass that is half full and not the one that is half empty. Encouraging children to 'look on the bright side of life' helps them be positive and keeps them happier.

Don't do too much for your children

Have a balance of things they need to take responsibility for and things you will do for them. Praise your child for wanting to be independent and responsible.

Encourage more play activities

Children learn through play and giving them real play opportunities will develop their skills and make them feel happy. Outdoor games, away from sedentary activities like watching television, is good for their physical and mental growth.

Share your evening meal together

This is a wonderful way to connect with the family. Everyone can share about their day and just enjoy being a family together. Talking about gratitude develops appreciation for their things even small things, from children. Mom and dad can be good role models at this time.

Practice gratitude

Knowing how to be grateful for even the little things you have contributes enormously to your own happiness. Sharing these gratitude comments with the family make everyone aware of gratitude and how to value the things and people around you.

Set boundaries and use positive parenting skills

Positive Parenting skills are linked to discipline. The kind of discipline that is part of the training you're giving your child to improve their happiness and give them opportunities to develop and reach their physical, cognitive, emotional, and social milestones.

Discipline, in a positive parenting style of raising children, is the backbone to your successful, happy child. Discipline is not about punishment, but about training. Thinking of discipline as training, makes your understanding of discipline different. Discipline is part of the steps you take to raise your children as responsible adults. Sometimes you may feel frustrated because your style of discipline is not working. Remember every child is different. What worked for one child may not work for others. Whatever worked at one age may not work with older children. Every so often it may be necessary to review disciplinary actions.

What to do when discipline is not working

You may be feeling frustrated, annoyed, or just defeated if your discipline is not working. What can you do to fix the situation without just throwing your arms in the air and saying, 'I give up, do it your way!'

Look at three simple suggestions to help you through difficult times and overcome a feeling that your discipline is not effective.

1. Don't give up too soon.

It is importation to try to stick to what you have put in place with regard to your disciplinary boundaries. If children do get their way too soon, they see themselves as winning the battle. They immediately see a loophole in your training. The smart toddler will use that same tactic to get their own way every time. It could be whining, crying, and rolling on the floor or sulking. Try to distract your toddler and move on. Sometimes it is just a power struggle emerging and a distraction does the trick. It helps you avoid any further clashes. You can go back to the original problem later.

2. The consequences you set are not working.

You have consequences in place, but they are not working.

What are your consequences really about? Are they more geared to a punishment? Review your consequences and if there is a pattern forming of the same things happening in spite of the consequences, perhaps there is room for learning a lesson or being shown how to put things right.

3. Don't take your discipline upset personally.

Your child is not specifically getting back at you each time there is a problem. The stubborn streak could be part of a bigger picture and a learning curve your toddler is going through. Try and relate to the situation and have empathy. Get down to your toddlers' level and work things out together. It may be as simple as respecting they were in the middle of a game and if you just empathize with the fact they were playing, or had set something out for later, then together you can work out a tidy up strategy.

A necessary element to learning lessons early on in your child's growing process is to have a desire to learn new things. Children are naturally curious and if you point them in the right direction and encourage natural curiosity, they should develop a love of learning.

Why a love of learning is important to teach.

Teaching children to love learning arouses a sense of curiosity at an early age. It is one of the ingredients that help with growing a happy child. Through a love of learning children begin to be more interested in change and discovering new things. A love of learning can start early on in your child's life and tap into the toddler's natural curiosity. A love of learning is part and parcel of the desire to explore and discover new things.

Here are some of the conditions that encourage a love of learning.

- There is a meaningful reason to want to do something. For example, your toddler may love to play with blocks and build

a tower because they are learning about the size and shape of the blocks and how to balance them.
- The learning conditions vary sometimes and become more daring or exciting. There is an added dimension to the learning. Using an example of the blocks and adding a train set or toy cars to run under block bridges adds a difference to the learning with blocks.
- The learning process is sociable and part of a game. you're joining in to help learn with the blocks. Your presence makes it sociable and encourages a love of learning.

In this way, just the simple act of playing with blocks, and looking at three suggestions to encourage a love of learning, the activity has become more meaningful and fun.

Growing pains seem to be a really real part of growing up. At the age of two going onto the teens tantrums can be expected. They are part of growing up. The question parents ask often is how do they survive these years from the tantrums to the outcome they wish to see and nurture of the 'extremely, happy kid.

Is this just an impossible task? Parents do want to know can they aspire to leaving tantrums behind and realizing they have actually raised an extremely happy kid!

First of all, it is important to acknowledge that tantrums are part of growing up and toddlers do have them. The terrible twos is a real phase of your child's life. The intensity of the tantrum, and the length of time they last, is different with each child. They are most common between the ages of 1 – 3 years.

The intensity of your child's tantrum can be anything from crying, screaming, kicking out, throwing their arms around, or falling on the floor. More intense tantrums can result in vomiting, holding their breath, and becoming aggressive and breaking things. However, your toddler manifests his or her tantrum, it comes as a shock to parents, and is upsetting for everyone.

Tantrums are the result of insecurities and frustrations due to immature social and emotional skills. Toddlers are trying to manage their feelings and trying to experience some independent life. They are discovering they can have an effect, through their behavior, on other people.

There are certain triggers and knowing these can help avert the chance of a tantrum.

- Stress factors like hunger, being over tired, or over stimulated can all lead to a tantrum. Being out of routine may cause toddlers to feel stress.
- Temperament plays a part, especially with children who have a volatile temper. The influence of temperament is part of who your child is. Your child may have more temper outbursts than other children. Learning how to manage these outbursts, and the triggers for setting them off, is part of knowing and understanding your child.
- Strong emotions, that they are not able to monitor, can set off a temper tantrum. These emotions would be worry, anger, fear, and embarrassment.
- Frustration comes when there is something they want or if

another child has taken something precious to them. This causes a tantrum and they become angry when they cannot get their things back. It is usually because they do not have the words to say what they mean.

If you could write a recipe to produce the happiest kid what would your ingredients be?

Plenty of playtime

Children learn through play. This is the most positive and important ingredient to growing a happy well-balanced child. Physical play, creative play, imaginative play, and cognitive activities along with social play opportunities all help with child development.

Routine and sleep

Children thrive in a routine of daily activities like mealtimes, bath time and sleep times. These routine times contribute to their sense of security.

Healthy meals

A well-balanced diet is a very important ingredient. A healthy diet with fruit and vegetables, plenty of water, and not too many sweets or soda drinks, will keep your child well-nourished and growing a healthy body and mind.

Freedom to express emotions

Being able to say how you feel and receive empathy towards your feelings helps children to be able to deal with difficult situations with more depth of understanding. It enables them to share in the feelings of others too.

Family values

Creating values for your family and putting them into practice helps children feel rooted in something bigger than themselves. Parents need to be sharing these values and showing their children how they uphold the family values.

Gratification

This is one of the most important ingredients to creating a happy life. Knowing what you're grateful for, and expressing it every day is what build up the moral and happiness factor in your child's life. Gratitude can be expressed every day. The dinner table or any family mealtime is a good time and place to express gratitude.

Voices that are heard

These are not the voices you hear in your head! The voices of your child as he/she tries to tell you about an emotion or an event in their lives are the voices to be heard. It may take your toddler a long time to say what they need to say but take the time out to be a good listener and hear those little voices.

Unconditional love

Unconditional love is the amazing love you give in good times and bad. It is a deep love that makes allowance for mistakes and forgives many mishaps. Unconditional love is not a weak and fickle love that may change along the way. It is the kind of love that nurtures and provides a happy harmonious nurturing environment filed with security for a child.

This recipe has no measures. The successful outcome relies on constant mixing of the ingredients and balancing the right mixture as needs arise. This recipe is not guaranteed to give instant success but persevere in providing a diet of these important ingredients and the outcome should be a healthy happy child.

How to prepare, mix together and produce your happy kid in all kinds of circumstances.

- Start with a secure and nurturing bowl called home.
- Add healthy food and a stable routine of sleep and family time.
- Mix in family values and plenty of gratification.
- Let the mixture rest while voices are heard.
- And feelings appreciated.
- Top up with more time to play as the mixture for your happy kid proves itself.
- Allow freedom of expression as you knead and mix this happy kid recipe together.
- Finally remember to coat your happy kid with mountains of unconditional love.

This coating of unconditional love is the magic ingredient that brings out the best in every child. It gives them the security and confidence to be the best they can be.

AA Milne, in his stories about Winnie the Pooh and Piglet, summed up the right attitude to unconditional love. Pooh asked Piglet how to spell love. The answer was:

"You don't spell love, you feel it."

A child who feels unconditional love will be the happiest child around.

CONCLUSION
YOU WIN - YES TO THE BEST

In conclusion, do you feel you can say yes to success? Has this book transformed your idea of parenting? Are you ready to continue your parenting journey feeling guilt free?

Did you know, that according to Albert Schweitzer, Nobel Peace prize winner, humanitarian and medical missionary,

> "Success is not the key to happiness.
> Happiness is the key to success!"

Happiness then is the essence of a well-balanced child and successful parenting.

The aim of this unique book on parenting is to bring about that kind of success. It is a realistic guide that takes you through different aspects of positive parenting.

The introduction, and getting to know your toddler, is relevant to finding your concept of parenting skills. Developmental milestones help parents with their expectations of their young children. An honest SWOT analysis, of your own experiences in parenting, is aimed at helping the reader to dig deep into their own capabilities as they are encouraged to adopt sound parenting skills.

Taking a SWOT analysis of your parenting skills at the beginning of the book was planned to give parents a realistic check up on their approach to parenting. It was an objective discussion point to evaluate what you as a parent would get out of the chapters on positive parenting and the inclusion of potty training.

What did you discover about yourself in relation to positive parenting? Knowing as a parent you have strengths to build on is encouraging. Facing some possible weak areas enables you to self-correct and look for new parenting possibilities. When you have an objective concept of what you bring to the parenting table you're more open to new ideas. This current generation of parents, with modern technology, and many more opportunities for help and advice is conscious of wanting more. Parents today do not want to parent in the same way as they were raised. The new ideals and suggestions, made to suit the mantra of positive parenting, makes this book stand out as something for the needs of current parenting expectations.

The aim of this book is to enlighten and encourage the reader to adopt positive parenting skills and raise a happy and successful child. The book does not imagine parenting is a solo performance. It talks about lighthouses. These are the beams of hope offered through building relationships with others and having a dependable book to refer to.

One of the greatest qualities known to parenting is patience. Patience follows through at every opportunity in this book. The analogy of raising a chicken, through hatching an egg, and not by smashing it to pieces, is a good one. Eggs are fragile and need love and care. In the same way positive parenting relies on nurturing, with love and patient interaction. This philosophy is carried through the different stages of child development.

Practical help is offered through knowing your personal parenting threshold, based on your personality type. There are added guidelines for how and when to seek for professional help. You do not have to be in this parenting game alone.

The chapter on looking for the right daycare facility, or for a caregiver, is very helpful. If you're a parent needing support while you go back to work, this chapter is invaluable. There are guidelines with the right questions to ask as you evaluate a possible care facility. Knowing what to look for, in your child's best interest, will give you peace of mind while your child is at the day care or nursery school. The stakes are high in the daycare world. You should expect only the best teamwork for your child while you have them looked after and educated at the same time. Early childhood education is vital to your child's foundational phase of learning. Do not compromise on this phase. This book advises you to be sure the daycare you choose meets the suggested criteria.

Then there is potty-training. Many parents dread the potty-training routine. Several chapters on potty training sincerely help parents with this big milestone. Potty-training is in fact all about readiness and patience from parents and the child concerned. Many parents find potty-training a real challenge. Toddlers can dig their heels in and rebel against any kind of training. It is comforting to know there are developmental stages and learning curves that affect potty-training. The section in this book that deals with potty-training, maps out different methods of introducing the potty, and this is reassuring. Parents may choose the one they feel most comfortable with. If that method does not work, there is no harm in taking a break and trying another method.

Providing a two in one book approach makes this book extra relative to positive parenting. Learning about potty-training, and working hand in hand with the positive guilt free direction given in these chapters, is really helpful. Parents can approach various parent issues and added to that have support with how to potty train their toddler.

One of the unique qualities of this book on parenting is the caring commentary and encouraging helpful points given throughout each chapter. There is positive recognition for individuality and catering for different needs. Early on in the initial chapters the book recognizes not only are children unique and individual, but so are the parents raising these unique beings.

This is the kind of parenting book you will want to read over again to take advantage of the constructive advice and genuine empathy with the challenges of parenting. It is a book encouraging parents to be positive and really care about finding solutions to parenting problems.

Dr Seuss, shares wisdom on parenting through his children's books and says:

> *"Unless someone like you cares a whole, awful lot,*
> *Nothing is going to get better. It is not.*
> *And will you succeed? Yes indeed, yes indeed!*
> *Ninety-eight and three-quarters percent guaranteed."*

Now take that caring message to heart and know, yes indeed, this book is just the support you need and with patience and parental love, you're guaranteed to succeed!

POSITIVE PARENTING & EDUCATING WITHOUT SHOUTING (2 IN 1)

HOW TO RAISE A HAPPY & EMOTIONALLY HEALTHY CHILD USING PROVEN STRATEGIES, UNCONDITIONAL LOVE & SHAME FREE DISCIPLINE

INTRODUCTION

Would you ever consider flying in a plane with only one wing? You are probably looking at this page in horror! Who in their right mind would ever consider getting in a plane with one wing? A plane with one wing would not get very far. Two wings balance and steady the plane. Wilbur Wright, with his brother Orville of the Wright brothers fame who flew the first plane ever, said:

> "It is possible to fly without motors, but not without knowledge and skill."
>
> — WILBUR WRIGHT

Exactly the same can be said about parenting. Like a plane with two wings, parenting needs two support systems. Successful parenting is guided through the <u>knowledge</u> of child development and the <u>skill</u> of positive parenting. A positive parenting plane ride using unconditional love and guilt free discipline.

There is a French proverb that says,

> 'There is no flying without wings,'

The same is true about parenting. It is the proverbial wings of knowledge and skill that act as wings to support the flight path of the parenting plane. A flight, not without turbulence, as you navigate the highs and lows of your growing child's development.

This book aims to take you, the reader, on a flight full of fantastic enlightening parenting skills. Like the plane with two wings the skills will be balanced with knowledge and insight into relevant child development phases to reach your goal. The goal of having a happy, emotionally healthy child. Through the knowledge you gain from this book you will be able to develop your own guilt free discipline methods. The knowledge you acquire will help you build the two wings of your parenting plane. The knowledge of how children grow and develop will give you more understanding of the mental, physical and emotional abilities your child has. The guidelines in this book help you to develop the yin and the yang of parenting.

Yin and Yang shows us how to create two parts to make a whole. Opposites but the parts that compete the whole in harmony. The key to happy parenting is harmony. In the yin and Yang philosophy, day balances night to make the whole twenty-four hours of time. Here are other halves that make the whole through their contrasts.

- Difficult and easy complement each other.
- High and low oppose one another.
- Long and short define one another.
- Fore and aft follow each other

In parenting, parent and child raise one another through unconditional love and discipline.

Raising children through positive connections and communication is a rewarding experience. Never without its challenges, but with room to grow, parenting is an experience to be cherished. Like the dualism of yin and yang there are many interesting parallels through this journey.

Aviators use these words of wisdom to define flight. These are their three key words

AVIATE, NAVIGATE, COMMUNICATE.

- **Aviate** – fly the plane.
- **Navigate** – steer the plane in the right direction.
- **Communicate** – interact and build relationships to help you along the way.

Your flight into parenting will need ground control, air traffic control, navigators, and passengers as well as a captain. Everyone involved has a common goal. A smooth flight and the joy of reaching their destination.

As you read through this book bear in mind the supportive role of knowledge through child developmental milestones and skills through learning how to parent. There is no standard plane that is going to convey you on this journey and the passengers, your children, will have different personalities and agendas. Ultimately you will all be trying to go in the same direction.

How does this book differ from other similar parenting books? The balance between understanding your child's growth patterns, and finding the skills to encourage and support them is the essence of this book. There is recognition of inevitable difficulties along the way. Parents are made aware of some of the things that are challenging for children at particular times in their lives simply because they have not reached that particular milestone. This kind of knowledge will help with tolerance through the turbulence. It gives you more understanding towards the troublesome two-year-old having temper tantrums, not because he/she wants to be disobedient, but because they are completely frustrated at that time without the language skills to communicate with you.

Positive connection and communication help parents to set healthy boundaries and realistic guidelines to their parenting. These boundaries are based on knowledge and are linked to the skills they need for parenting. As a result of this connection, coming from a loving place, parents will be on the path to raising a happy, self-disciplined child. This is the opportunity you have been looking for to transform your parenting styles and watch your child grow and mature in front of your very eyes.

Unconditional love will be the fuel for your plane. You will set a flight path towards a goal of having a happy, positive child, while you find your yin and yang of parenting. Fasten your seat belts and get ready for a give and take experience, one with highs and lows, never an open and shut case, but one of opportunities to encourage a sweet Jekyll and suppress Mr. Hyde. A dualism, like yin and yang will resonate well with parenting and the two wings of your parenting plane.

Even if your child is misbehaving 24/7 currently, even if you can't help but react with yelling, shouting, outbursts and even if you've tried the whole 'positive parenting' thing before and it didn't work, this book will outline STEP BY STEP how you can transform your parenting style, become the parent you want to be and watch your child's behavior change in front of your eyes.

It's time to break free from reactive parenting, give your child the unconditional love & support they need & raise the happiest child around! Put an end to that nagging guilt/shame you often feel after an outburst or yelling at your child.

So, If you want the blueprint to loving, compassionate parenting that radically transforms your child's behavior and raises the happiest child around, then this is the parenting book for you.

PART I

1

STARTING THE JOURNEY IN HARMONY

Yin and Yang, symbols of how all things exist as inseparable and contradictory opposites, have deep meaning in a parenting journey. The opposites complement one another. They bring a balance between each other to achieve harmony. Yin and Yang show us that opposing forces can co-exist and even rely on one another. This philosophy is a great one to apply to parenting. Parents learn from each other and need each other to bring different qualities to their parenting. Mother and father may comfort one another, or challenge one another, to provide the right environment to nurture healthy, happy children.

'Be prepared,' is a slogan that fits well with starting out on any journey, including a parenting journey. There are many words of wisdom to guide and encourage. Practical advice makes the most sense and here are three basic and practical positive parenting tips to start the journey.

THE 3 MUST-KNOW THINGS YOU CAN IMPLEMENT TODAY TO START YOUR POSITIVE PARENTING JOURNEY.

- Consistent parenting is key.
- Always get to the root of the problem.
- Be ready to discipline, that is to teach, not punish.

Within those three statements are three key words to take note of.

Be...**CONSISTENT**...find the...**ROOT**...**TEACH** the child.

<u>Consistent</u> parenting is absolutely vital. This is where the yin and yang of parenting comes to the fore and the parents bring together their different strengths and skills, but in a harmonious pattern, that leads to consistent parenting.

One of the most important aspects of parenting is setting boundaries and planning your family's core values. The boundaries and values are the ground rules that set the bar at the right height for consistent parenting. Boundaries give everyone a sense of belonging and they give parents the definition of the family and how it should behave. Boundaries and family values are intertwined and bring a sense of security and love to the family. Boundaries help with bringing about the yin and yang sense of drawing opposites together for the well-being of everyone.

<u>Root</u> knowledge, and understanding what is at the basis of problems, helps enormously with positive parenting. In every situation there is

an underlying reason for the problem. Applying sound knowledge, or digging deeper to find the root cause, is a very helpful parenting tool. Often parents assume their child is being unreasonable or difficult when the root of the problem may be the child has not reached the appropriate developmental milestone. This contributes to another yin and yang aspect of parenting. The behavior and the developmental stage reached by each child. When these two parts to parenting are in harmony with one another, parenting is made easier. Parents can use this knowledge to get to the root cause of many problems. Physical, emotional, social, and cognitive development are all important contributors to child development.

Teaching and learning how to grow through different situations helps children to develop in the right direction. Discipline is an important part of parenting, but the kind of discipline that teaches without heavy handed punishments is the kind of discipline that boosts children's morale and confidence. This kind of teaching falls in well with getting to the root of a problem and being consistent in the way the discipline is delivered. Children grow to trust their parents through this consistent root learning.

This quote is one to consider in the discipline and parenting niche. Written by Jim Rohn an entrepreneur and motivational speaker.

"Discipline is the bridge between goals and accomplishments."

— JIM ROHN

Goals are set with your family values and the boundaries surrounding them. The discipline you use to teach your children from a young age, leads to the successful accomplishment of raising happy and well-adjusted children.

These five basic steps will help you begin to engage with the parenting theory of positive parenting through guilt free discipline. Through having clear boundaries, consistent discipline and spending quality time with your child, you will learn the value of clear communication and building loving lasting relationships.

Here are five steps to take to realize that goal.

Step One:

Setting Boundaries.

Boundaries are all about respecting the needs of others and knowing what your needs are. Setting boundaries affects the way you look at your own personal space. An important part of setting and respecting boundaries is having empathy. Without empathy it is very difficult to see the need for boundaries and to follow them.

What sort of boundaries are appropriate you may ask? They are the guidelines that protect us physically, emotionally, and socially. They do change as we and our children grow older, but the basic element of a boundary is to say, 'this far and no more' and why. It is the why part of the boundary that comes through learning about empathy. Finally, boundaries can only be respected if there are consequences to breaking these boundaries. The boundaries and the consequences need to be fully understood by everyone in the family.

Step Two:

<u>Having Consistent Discipline.</u>

Consistent discipline means parents react in the same way to situations needing discipline. There is no overreaction in some scenarios and no ignoring of something that was a major issue the day before. Parents will react and follow through in the same way each day. Parenting with consistent discipline creates an atmosphere of security and reduces anxiety. Children become accountable for their choices because they know there is a consistent line of discipline.

Consistency is not easy. There are many pitfalls and at times you the parent will not want to stick to the boundaries you have set because you may be tired, or feeling different emotions yourself. However, being consistent eventually makes keeping your parenting and family values intact easier.

Here are some of the traps you may fall into that will upset your determination to be consistent.

Reacting emotionally

Emotional reactions are bound to be inconsistent. React with anger and you will flare up and be unpredictable. Try to get in touch with the emotion before you react and then give your child a calm and composed response. Take some deep breaths and remember your consistent discipline boundary.

Making idle threats

Threats without consequences do not help children to learn about consistent discipline. When you make the boundaries that are part of your discipline make sure the behavior you expect is in line with the expectations you have of the children.

Wanting to please your child in every situation

No parent wants to be the 'bad cop' all the time giving out the punishments and monitoring behavior. Remember children do need a parent they respect. Trying to be the good guy and your child's buddy is not filling the role of a parent.

Too much talk and not enough action

Threatening to act on something that is considered wrong behavior and nagging continually will not result in showing your children consistent discipline.

Keeping your focus on the wrong doings of children and not looking at their good behavior

Remember to highlight good behavior as well as the things that cross the boundary set out as part of your family's code of conduct. Give loads of praise for good behavior.

Let your no be no

Sometimes it is challenging to maintain your response of NO. It is important to retain this decision to stick to a no response. Try say:

'We will think about that,' or 'maybe' instead of an outright no and then not being able to stick to that.

Playing parents off against one another

Children can be very good at this. Don't fall into the trap of being played off against your parenting partner. Stand firm and stand together.

One of the most important things about consistent discipline is sticking together as parents. When both parents are standing by one another the consistent discipline is a whole lot easier.

The song "Stand by Me" comes to mind when thinking about parents who stick together.

> *Stand by me,*
> *(part of the lyrics say)*
> *If the sky we look upon,*
> *Should tumble and fall*
> *Or the mountain should crumble to the sea*
> *I won't cry, I won't cry*
> *No, I won't shed a tear*
> *Just as long as you stand by me.*

When parents stand together the challenges of parenting are lighter, and they have a partner to stand with in times of difficulty.

Step Three:

Spend Quality Time with your Kids.

Quality time with your kids may seem like an impossible task when you already have a very busy schedule. Added to that, children today have busy schedules too. How do you get to spend quality time together? Well, you have to plan for it and even if it is a short period of time it has to be quality time! Not time where you spend half your time focused on your phone or engaged in another activity. Quality time is classified as one of our love languages. If you are going to pass on love through time with your child, it needs to be the quality you would expect.

Here are some suggestions of ways to spend quality time with your child.

- Schedule regular dates with your child. The nature of the date will depend on the age and interest of the child. The point is to arrange a special time with your child. Go for a walk together, make cookies together, buy ice creams or watch a movie. All these ideas could fill the slot of a date together.
- Make extra time for some quality story time in your bedtime routine. Leave time for talking about your day and finding out what kind of day your child had too.
- Exercise or walk together. Take time out of your day to do some exercise together or depending on your child's age go walking together. Go to the park and enjoy watching your child run and jump and climb too before you go home.

- Organize a camp out or picnic in the garden. Preparing for this kind of family activity and taking pictures of the event is a way of bonding and spending quality time.
- A family movie night is another activity with popcorn and all the real movie treats to spend time together as a family. Yes, there is a movie on, but make a point of watching together, and talk about the movie at the end.
- Depending on the age of your children family games night is another way of spending quality time together. Bring out a family favorite and enjoy the competition.

Step Four:

Learn how to communicate with each other.

Communication is all about listening and talking to your children. When you get this right, you have a better chance of fostering positive parent and child relationships.

Communication channels are opened with your child from birth. Providing a safe environment with gentle responses to your baby's early sounds begins that close sense of bonding you need for meaningful communication.

Here are some tips to take into account for early communication:

- Give your baby or toddler your full attention through your body language and the gentle sounds you make.
- Encourage listening and responding to all kinds of things.

Good and bad, angry or calm interactive communication is important.
- Help your child to share their feelings as this will help you understand them better.
- Make time for actually talking to one another. Mealtimes are the perfect times for family discussions.
- Switch off all distractions so you can focus on each other.
- Be aware of your child's body language. Often there are signs something is not quite right before your child has started to speak.
- Active listening is a key aspect of good communication.

Active listening may be a skill parents need to learn, and this is what it means with regard to parenting.

Body language is important. This means you show by your facial expressions and eye contact that you are really listening. You need to watch your child's facial expressions in return for anxiety, confusion or anger. Their faces will also express joy and excitement.

Practice building on to what they are saying with words of encouragement like, 'really' or goodness please tell me more. Rephrasing what your child has said is another way of adding to the communication between you. Let your child finish what they are saying and try not to cut off their story. Help with empathy and bringing out what you or they may have been feeling.

Parents need to remember communication is not only about giving instructions. Sometimes it is easy to forget that telling children what to do all the time is not really communication. That is more instruction. Healthy happy communication helps to strengthen your relationship with your child. When you are always just giving instructions, your child may just switch off and not really want to hear what you have to say.

Try these suggestions to open the doors to better communication.

- Make a point of leading conversations to require more than a one-word answer.

   Say things like:
   - *Oh, that was amazing tell me more...*
   - *Wow how interesting so what happened next?*
   - *I see and how did you feel after that...*

- Try to use positives in conversation like please do this or that not always don't do something. Don't is negative and stops conversation.
- Think about using the first person I in conversation not you.

You are very untidy becomes I need you to tidy up your room.

Or you need to have better table manners becomes I need you to eat nicely with a knife and fork. Take the accusing word you off the focus of the child.

- Don't label children or say unkind words to their face. Telling children they are being bad or shaming them with derogatory labels is not good for their morale or communication with you.

- Let your child know they are loved and accepted, it is the behavior you dislike and not the child in times of discipline. This will in turn let your child feel good about themselves and want to please you more. This opens lines of communication between you.

Step five:

Compliment where you can.

The simple act of praise builds your child's confidence and helps them to see what they are good at. Praising behaviors you like is good for character building. Parents can successfully praise children at different ages for the stages of development they are at during that particular phase. This is where knowing the appropriate milestones helps with selecting the right kind of praise. For example, praise for potty training goes hand in hand with the toddler phase. Praise for sharing might fit with starting preschool or the arrival of a new sibling. Praise for homework and good grades goes with primary school and so on.

Giving and receiving compliments goes a long way to building relationships. Compliments that praise character are ones that help towards building that character. These compliments improve your child's feeling of personal self-worth. Compliments help to bring out the best in children.

Now you are armed with these five basic steps to positive parenting you have a benchmark to use when you come to take stock of your own parenting skills. In chapter two you are going to take an audit of your parenting style. Even if you are a first-time parent you will have some idea of what parenting means. Where did you get those ideas, and will you be putting them into practice?

An audit is all about balancing. Jill Wagner, actress, television personality and model with a great work ethic has said:

> "I always do a mental audit at the end of the week to make sure I'm balancing time between my career and my personal life."
>
> — JILL WAGNER

Apply this to your parenting life and get the balance right between positive parenting and developmental psychology.

2

TAKING STOCK OF YOUR PARENTING STYLE BEFORE YOU START

Taking stock or auditing your parenting potential before you start this next chapter is a good idea. The checks and balances of parenting or any activity you embark on will make a difference to the outcome and the results you aspire to.

The balance of parenting is often about getting connection and independence right. The dualism of highs and lows. Every action in your parenting lifestyle is not necessarily going to be a high note. Balancing parenting skills is a challenge, and every parent is faced with the ultimate parenting question.

HOW DO I KNOW WHAT IT MEANS TO BE A PARENT?

There are four sources most people use to reference parenting skills. Parenting does not come with a regular handbook. Children are not born with a book of instructions. Most prospective parents turn to these four sources for parenting knowledge. Once you have assessed these parenting sources then you can audit the skills you have gained from them and have an objective look at what you think will serve you well, and what you should modify, or just discard.

FOUR SOURCES OF PARENTING SKILLS ARE:

1. We learn from our parents

We may have had awesome parents with all the qualities one would want to emulate. Our home life may have been the happiest most perfect in every way and the one we would want to have for our children. On the other hand, there may be flaws in our upbringing that we do not wish to bring into our own family life. Either way our parents will have taught us something about parenting. When there are two parents in the parenting partnership there are two sets of experiences, cultures, and traditions in the mix. Traditional parenting styles may not resonate well in today's world. Parenting today needs more guidance due to technology and more pressure on families to perform in the faster pace of this century.

2. Parenting can be learned from books, magazines, and articles on parenting

There is a wealth of information available on parenting. It is difficult to decide on what to read with all the choices out there. Find a style that fits in with your family life and be open to suggestions and ideas. Try out the ideas you feel you can manage based on your family values. Having a goal in mind gives you the direction you need. Finding a parenting publication to enable you to reach that goal helps to sift through the various types of advice. Getting an overall view through a complete book helps initially. Then find extra help on specifics like potty training or sleep patterns, as well as diet and food information. All these types of advice will help build a parenting profile, but having a goal in mind will keep you focused.

3. We watch our friends with their families

There is nothing quite as consoling as watching people you know well handle their children. Seeing good parenting in action helps new parents feel they are not alone in this experience. They have fellow parents to talk to. Close friends or siblings who are actively involved in parenting are a comforting option to ask for advice. They may have the perfect answer for your problem and will be empathetic at the same time. Friends can point you in the right direction if you need some professional help. You will feel you are on the same page with friends who are parenting at the same time as you are.

4. Parenting can be learned from our children as we learn on the job

There is nothing like learning as you go. When your children arrive, you will have to tailor make your parenting to suit their needs and your family life. It really is a hands-on, practical experience and you will feel you have been thrown in at the deep end. One of the best pieces of advice is to have parenting goals and boundaries that reflect your values. This gives you the foundation to your parenting. It is a point of reference for balancing your parenting act.

Learning life lessons from our children is likened to looking in a mirror.

Dr Christina Hibbert wrote:

> *Our children are mirrors.*
> *Through them we see our flaws*
> *Our mistakes our humanity.*
> *Through them we see our*
> *Strengths, our gifts, our deep abiding love.*
> *The best and the worst in us*
> *Reflect as we parent.*
> *As we pay attention to these*
> *Reflections, we learn, we improve.*
> *And we grow.*

YES, PARENTING IS ALL ABOUT GROWTH.

When you audit your parenting skills these are some of the points to check and balance your performance against. This check list is here to guide with the knowledge that every family is unique. Reflecting on these skills is meant to improve personal growth and not to judge.

Parenting skills for your check list

1. Giving love and affection in a supportive manner

This may seem pretty obvious. Parents love their children right? Yes, they do, but the skill to check here is in a supportive manner. Parents may be demonstrative showing hugs and mountains of physical affection. This is great, but what can parents do that shows love in a supportive manner. This goes deeper than just the hugs and kisses.

Here are some suggestions if you feel your supportive love is lacking.

- Tell your child when you think they are doing something well. Thank them and say what it is that they are doing well.
- Spend time with them reading stories, playing games, listening to music, making something together or going on an outing.
- Thank them for being so wonderful, or doing something you appreciated and found helpful.
- Make bedtime that special time of the day when you appreciate one another and end the day on a positive note.
- Create memories together through your family traditions or starting a new family bonding time.
- Prioritize some one-on-one time with your child. This is especially meaningful if you have more than one child.
- Be enthusiastic and show how excited you are about things your child is motivated about. Be ready to join in and support these activities.

2. Building relationships

Spending quality time with your child, and building trust, are two important factors linked to building relationships. In your audit of parenting balances have you checked on the amount of quality time you spend with your child? Does your child trust you on a day-to-day basis?

Relationships are built, that means they do not just happen. Quality time with a child helps to build the relationship as parent and child bond with each other. Bonding leads to trust and over time children learn to trust their parents.

Here are some suggestions of ways to build relationships.

- Listen to your child and show empathy. Try to understand things from your child's point of view. Connection with your child often starts with being a good listener.
- Play games together. Children learn through play and when you join in their play routines you will become part of their world.
- Have mealtimes together. Getting together as a family at mealtimes is one of the best times to build on family relationships.
- Set aside some one-on-one time free of distractions. This does not have to be a great length of time, but it does need to be quality time, of just the two of you together.
- Read books with your child. There are amazing stories to read on all sorts of topics, fantasy stories and good old-fashioned stories with morals and lessons to learn together.
- Show you love and value your child. Just the simple act of touch and showing affection is a perfect way to build a loving, trusting relationship.

3. Showing your child how to become independent

Independence is definitely something children can learn, and they only learn this skill if their parents allow them to do things for themselves. When parents do everything for their children the message they put across is they don't have confidence in their children to become independent. Take a look at your parenting to date. How much independence have you been encouraging? Start with small things and help your child to follow through with whatever they were doing independently. Use little home chores but make sure they are age appropriate.

Try some of these ideas to help your child with independence.

- Make a list of things your child could be doing by themselves. Start with things around the house like brushing teeth or making their own bed and gradually increase the activity level and the range of independence.
- Get your child to finish what they are expected to do and then praise their achievement.
- Give them household chores they can manage that impact on the whole family.
- Encourage them to play with younger siblings or friends' children so they get to see how mature they are in comparison, and that they can take on responsibility.
- When they reach school age let them make and pack their school lunch and bag. If they leave something behind don't run after them let them feel the responsibility of looking after themselves in this small way.

- Have a routine at home that they must stick to and be accountable for.
- Let your child make some choices and then see them follow through with their decision.
- Encourage your child to solve their own problems. Let them know you are there for guidance, but there are some things they could work out themselves.

4. Providing Education and Helping your Child to Learn

This is a big point to check on your audit. Providing education is not just about finding the right school. It is about teaching life skills and offering pathways to learning. Learning comes with good role modeling too. Does your child see that learning is important to you and to your family?

Here are some of the ways you can provide education and learning to your child.

- Try to start early because your child is ready to learn at a young age. This does not mean you have to send them off to school, there are many things you can do to foster early learning even before your child is ready to go to school.
- Encourage reading and a love of books. Start out with picture books and shared times of 'reading' until your child has mastered the skill of reading for themselves.
- Find out what interests your child then focus on those interests. Children go through phases depending on what has

caught their fancy. Dinosaurs, pets, cars, fish you name it, there are many interesting choices to support.
- Find out what your child's learning style is. There are three main learning styles. Visual, auditory and anesthetic. Knowing which style your child favors will help them learn better.
- Play games to make learning fun and something you can join in. This is particularly applicable to younger learners.
- Be encouraging by being focused on what is being learned not on how well your child is doing at that particular task.
- Make every day a day to learn something. It doesn't have to be academic. It could be learning to bake or walk the dog. The key is learning to experience something new.

5. Stress management skills

Firstly, as a parent you need to recognize your child is suffering from some form of stress. Do you know the signs of stress and if you do are you able to help your child with managing these stress issues? We all experience stress at some point in our lives. It is the nature of the world we live in. In your personal stress audit do you feel you help your child with some stress management strategies, or do you just ignore stress and perhaps unknowingly add to it? There are many indicators that your child may be stressed. You will know when your child is showing unusual behavior like outbursts of tears, nail biting, bed wetting, loss of appetite, complaining of sore tummy and other physical signs of stress.

What can you do to help your child with their stress?

- Have a steady and practical routine at home that offers a healthy diet, good sleep patterns, and exercise.
- Keep their schedule simple. When there are extra events at school cut back on the schedule you have at home. Maintain a balance of activities.
- Make comments and ask your child how they are feeling. Keep lines of communication open to discuss any kind of stress.
- Make use of some relaxing processes. Depending on the age of your child teach them breathing exercises, walking and outdoor relaxation, yoga or listening to music. There are numerous ways to help your child relax during stressful times.

6. Helping your child to know how to keep safe

Our world grows daily in so many ways. Cities are huge, technology is advancing every day and children are exposed to much more than they were before. Parents need to help their children keep safe. As their children grow up, parents need to be ready to point out the dangers they may face and give them skills to cope with dangers.

What would be the best coping skills to share with your children?

- The most important factor in all the ways parents can help their children is to maintain a close relationship with your

child. Keep your child/parent relationship strong so your child knows they can depend on you in all circumstances.
- Teach personal safety rules from a young age. How to cross the road, avoiding talking to strangers, knowing who to trust or ask for help should they get lost, knowing their name and number to contact. These are all streetwise coping skills.
- Teach your child about personal body privacy. Tell them no one should touch them in private places or engage them in 'games' that are secret. Children are very vulnerable, and parents must teach them how to speak up if there is anything happening that they are not comfortable with.
- Safety clothing is very important, make helmets compulsory for any fast-moving outdoor sports. Seatbelts in cars for motor vehicle protection and teach your child to swim.
- Safety in the home environment. Your home can actually be a dangerous place for your child if you are not aware of practicing safety at home. Plugs, stoves, knives, medicine boxes, and strong cleaning chemicals all present dangers in your home. Anything that is dangerous for children especially the medicine box should be kept out of their reach. Teach them about plugs and hot things on the stove from an early age. There are plug covers and other safety in the home gadgets you can buy and when your child is ready to understand the reason for your NO is their safety house hazards become easier.

7. Providing positive discipline

Most of us have negative memories of discipline as we may have been raised in a strict family environment. However, today's parenting style has changed, and discipline is no longer about being the strict ogre, but trends today recognize the aspect of discipline that uses discipline as a teaching tool. Discipline is all about helping children learn and grow stronger to be well adjusted in life.

Follow these trends on positive parenting.

- Spend quality time with your child. At least fifteen minutes a day of QUALITY time is recommended as a positive parenting skill.
- Keep yourself informed about child development and try to learn new things about how your child is growing.
- Network with like-minded parents and friends. Join a support group to share ideas and help solve problems.
- Look after yourself by keeping a healthy lifestyle.
- Set out your family values and boundaries to assist with your parenting goals.

No one wants to fall into the bad parent trap. The main issues of bad parenting can be quantified into five observed categories. The reason for observing these areas is to use them as a balance between good and bad parenting and to turn the trends away from the bad towards the good. These five parenting areas are simply not negotiable when it comes down to parenting in a positive guilt free manner.

1. Withdrawing any signs of love or affection from a child.
2. Having little or no discipline whatsoever.
3. Shaming or labeling a child.
4. Having very rigid or strict discipline.
5. Not providing a safe caring home environment.

Each of these basic categories has different attributes, but together they add up to poor parenting and an unstable environment for children to grow up in.

In our world, good governance checks and balances have their place and are used to help reduce mistakes and prevent improper behavior. There is no harm done if you have a recon at home and look at your checks and balances. Your knowledge and practice of positive parenting should be growing. No one is perfect but keeping your eye on the goals and going forward is what makes your parenting journey positive.

"Life is like riding a bicycle. To keep your balance, you must keep moving."

— ALBERT EINSTEIN

Keep that quote in mind as you move on to the next chapters and learn more about child development and positive parenting.

3

BRAIN RESEARCH AND CHILD DEVELOPMENT

Did you know the brain is an amazing part of your child's body? It is the center of the body that commands everything else. At birth, the brain is, one quarter of the size it will become. The brain then doubles itself in the first year and keeps on growing rapidly. By the age of 3 it has reached 80% of its adult capacity. When your child gets to the age of 5 the brain is 90% of its total capacity. At birth a baby has all the brain cells or neurons it requires, but it is the process of connecting these cells, that really makes the brain work. During the connecting process the child learns to move, think, learn language, and reach different milestones. These are the building blocks your child needs to develop into a mature adult. It is clear from these growth patterns that the prime time for development is up to the age of five. These early years are the best time for developing higher order thinking skills, like problem solving, self-motivation, and communication.

You may be wondering how this growth actually works.

Everyday experiences, built through positive interaction with parents and care givers, contribute to this growth. These daily experiences determine which brain connections will develop and which ones will last for a lifetime. The infant, the first year of life, is when the baby begins to make this connection between the parents, the stimulation and the brain cells. When parents and caregivers interact positively with their child, they are literally building those connectors between brain cells. Simple activities of talking, reading, singing, and playing with children are crucial to the brain's development.

The brain is actually like a system of wires and connections. Messages are passed between the neurons of the brain and these reactions are called synapses. Science tells us that during the first three years the child's brain has nearly twice as many synapses as it will have during adulthood. The brain is working overtime during these first three years. The repeated use of synapses strengthens these connections. When the baby is born it can recognize the sound of its mother's voice and soon tells the difference between inanimate objects and its parents especially the mother figure.

The rapid development of motor skills in the first year are attributed to the growth of the cerebellum which triples in size. Language circuits are consolidated during the very busy first year as the frontal and temporal lobes of the brain grow. The child's first language and sounds are being imprinted on the brain. In the second year the brain develops cognitive abilities. Higher order thinking skills develop like self-awareness and emotions. When year three comes along the brain is understanding past and present tense and cognitive functions are improving daily. All this early brain development is the beginnings of so many thinking and speaking activities. However, there is a downside. If a child is exposed to negativity at this stage these experiences have a huge negative effect on their achievement and happiness.

Here are some interesting facts about the brain and early childhood development.

- The brain likes to build on repetitive experiences especially when the senses are involved.
- The brain enjoys music.
- Movement engages well with the brain.
- Stress does not encourage brain functions.
- The brain is making the most connections for growth and development while the child is very young.

What is going on as the brain develops and how can research help parents with their child's early years? Many parents are wanting answers to this question. If we look at three key areas the visual cortex, cerebellum and the myelination we can learn some of the intricacies of the brain. There is a great deal of activity happening in your infant's head!

Visual Cortex:

When the baby is born everything is a bit fuzzy, but by six months there is rapid growth and the baby can see depth perception, and their vision is nearly as clear as an adult. Letting your child see colors, shapes and movement helps them to develop these areas of vision.

Cerebellum:

From rolling over by themselves to crawling and walking your child has made rapid progress in their motor skills. This development comes through the cerebellum and it triples in size during this phase. Encouraging movement through using their arms and legs at this time helps to increase fine and gross motor skills.

The Myelination:

The nerve cells that allow for a faster transfer of brain signals helps the baby's brain to receive and transmit messages faster. These nerves are rapidly developing as the brain grows in size.

LET'S LEARN HOW BRAIN CONNECTIONS ARE DEVELOPED THROUGH PROVIDING A HEALTHY ENVIRONMENT.

Different environments and behaviors surrounding the infant and the toddler will affect their brain development. Knowing how to provide the best all round stimulation and atmosphere to grow in is a very important component to healthy brain development. Children grow through different types of interaction from the people around them. There are social interactions, physical development, encouraging cognitive development and language too. Children need to develop their senses, extend their memory and their powers of reasoning. The development of language is high on the list of interactive growth while the brain works with motor skills, emotional development and helps the child mature ready for formal learning.

Daniel J Siegel who wrote 'The Whole Brain Child.' had this to say about developing the brain

---

"As children develop, their brains 'mirror' their parent's brain. In other words, the parent's own growth and development, or lack of those, impact on the child's brain. As parents become more aware and emotionally healthy, their children reap the rewards and move forward toward health as well."

— DANIEL J SIEGEL

Here are 10 areas of growth that are taking place withing the realms of your baby's brain development. These areas meet the needs of their physical, mental, social, and emotional growth. In addition, there are some things to avoid during this time of extra special growth.

1. Nutrition:

Proper nutrition during early childhood development is closely linked to brain development. A healthy diet providing all the right proteins, vitamins, and minerals will help the brain to grow and develop naturally. While they say 'breast is best' for baby, mom needs to be properly nourished too. Make sure you have a healthy diet of eggs for protein, leafy greens and fish for omega 3 fatty acids. Mom needs lots of fluid too for breast feeding. Remembering how the brain is growing in those early years is a good way to trigger healthy eating habits.

2. Physical activity:

It is no surprise that a healthy brain stems from a healthy body. Exercise in early childhood can improve the infant's cognitive development. There are many activities that will enhance the physical and mental growth of the baby. Tummy time or lying on their tummy is a recommended activity. Tummy time strengthens the neck muscles and the stomach too.

3. Sensory development:

We all have five senses and through using our senses we interact with others and with the world around us. Seeing, hearing, touching, tasting, and smelling are the senses supported by the brain and exploring the world through their senses is part of brain development. Allow your child to get messy and muddy as part of sensory exploration. Have a sensory tray at home where you can put out different objects to encourage touching and sensory exploration. This should only be done when your child is able to touch and feel without putting everything into their mouths!

4. Social connection:

Neuroscience has provided incredible information about the social brain. The brain is able to recognize faces from an early age and through facial expressions understand how people feel. Understanding what people know and how they feel is an important part of cognitive development. The brain can tune into human voices and has an entire neural network just for learning language. This social side of the brain responds to all the senses too.

5. Emotional development:

This is an area of early childhood development where children have to grow as they mature. It is an important area of development sometimes known as emotional intelligence. The basis of emotional intelligence is empathy. Without empathy you cannot relate to emotions and understand how other people may feel. Through emotional intelligence children learn to understand why they are being rewarded or punished.

6. Developing logic:

Logic and abstract thinking are developmental stages in each and every child. There are some concepts they will not manage until they have reach specific developmental milestones. Helping children with recognizing patterns and building with blocks are great ways to start encouraging logic and perceptual skills. Finding differences in pictures and looking for hidden objects are another way of developing some logic and cognitive development.

7. Developing memory:

Memory skills and developing memory is a big part of the brain's function. The brain is capable of different types of memory. Having an ability to remember things is a skill that will serve you well in life, wherever you are and whatever your circumstances become. You can practice memory skills through games and listening to stories that you then have to recall. Developing memory is a worthwhile life skill.

- Short term memory is what you remember in the shortest time that the memory enters the brain. It is stored quickly.
- Working memory is what we use to remember how to do things. It helps us make decisions, solve problems and make everyday life decisions. Toddlers are developing this memory and will improve as they grow older.
- Explicit memory is the part of our memory that has collected experiences, memories, a memory of episodes in your life that you can access if you need to.
- Long term memory is the things you have experienced and remember for a long time.
- Autobiographical memory is the memory of episodes in your life that are personal and part of your memories.

8. Language development:

Here is an incredible piece of information. The baby's brain is already learning sounds, hearing voices, and learning the rhythm of language in the womb. Language development is one of the most important functions of the brain. At birth the baby is ready for communication. Starting with looking at you when you speak and then making their own cooing and gurgling noises. In the first four years of growth and development your child's language is going to increase from sounds and noises to words and sentences.

9. Motor skills – fine and gross motor development:

The control of large muscles needed for holding up their heads and crawling, leading up to walking, begin first. Then the fine motor skills follow on from here as your child grows more able to control fine motor exercise. Child specialists are very dedicated to the interaction between the developing brain and cognitive skills. There is a direct link between physical development and learning. Exercise strengthens the vital organs of the body, builds muscle tone and is directly connected to improved school grades.

10. Things to avoid for healthy development:

While the brain is involved in all these positive ways to grow and develop it is important to know some of the things that may affect the brain badly.

- Neglect, abuse, and traumatic experiences deeply affect the brain's development.
- Poor nutrition and lack of exercise lead to lack of stimulation and nurture for the brain.
- Pollution and impoverished living conditions have a negative effect on the growth of the brain in infants and young children.
- A poor diet, and the unhealthy lifestyle of the mother during pregnancy, affects the baby even before birth.

Knowledge of how the brain is developing and how it has an amazing capacity to grow makes parents all the more responsible during this vulnerable time to help their children to develop and optimize this growth period. Here are some simple interactions to have with your infant and toddler in the early phases of brain development to nurture and develop the growth of the brain's neurons.

It may seem like a contradiction of terms but play and learn are the basics of infant growth and stimulation of the brain. Children learn through play. Playing with your children and providing play resources and opportunities is the best way to stimulate your child in the first three years. Reading or looking at books is another vial intervention and through books language is stimulated as well as many learning experiences. Making sure your baby feels comforted and secure in their environment provides the stable environment need for growth. The brain is stimulated by the environment and parents and care givers are in a position to intervene and provide the right kind of environment for healthy brain growth.

Dr Seuss has this summed up in his simplistic quote:

"You have brains in your head and feet in your shoes.

You can steer yourself any direction you choose."

— DR SEUSS

Knowing how the brain is activated and is growing inside your child's head is a great incentive to parents to encourage that growth and give the child the opportunity to go any direction they choose.

4

IMPORTANCE OF THE FIRST FEW YEARS

Babies may look like cute little bundles of joy, ready to cuddle, lying and cooing in their cribs. They are adorable, but they are so much more than just a little bundle of fun. Babies, especially in their first year of life, are lying there housing a brain that is growing rapidly. The brain's success rate and growth are dependent on those very early years. The human brain grows with use and the number of neural connections a child gains are made up in those first years of the baby's life.

Did you know that movement is one of the most important experiences a baby can have? It is through movement that the brain is stimulated ready for more learning. There are lovely early movement programs that promote movement and learning at a very young age. In the first year of a baby's life, he/she will learn how to lift their heads, roll over from their backs to their tummies, sit and crawl, stand, and possibly walk. That in itself is a lot of movement, muscle control, balance and determination.

Movement in the first year helps the body and the brain connect and develop gross and fine motor skills that influence the sensory motor system and helps to develop the brain. Resisting gravity or pushing up against the floor is part of this growth through movement. It develops an understanding of where the child is in relation to the space they are part of. Another important part of movement is finding balance. These early movements and learning how to balance as the baby becomes more upright helps the brain to develop a vestibular system. The vestibular system is the sensory system providing a sense of balance and spatial orientation. This sense of space and balance is developed through movement. The body and the brain need to link with one another to prepare the infant for thinking and growing their brain capacity.

What can parents and care givers do at this crucial stage?

Yhis is a time of allowing babies opportunities to be rolling on a play mat, lifting their heads and spending valuable time rocking on their tummies. Babies and toddlers need to be exposed to outdoor play and toys they can explore with as they rattle or roll. Try taking children out more to play outdoors and to experience different aged appropriate activities. Try not to confine them to their baby chairs or playpens. Give them toys to push or pull and just encourage movement wherever possible. Playing with random objects that are safe for this age group is known as 'loose parts' play. Different shaped objects with different sizes and textures to explore make a wonderful selection of objects to interact with.

Here are some practical tips and development areas to help with your baby's brain development in the first year. You may be doing many of these things without realizing the significance of them. It helps to know you are on the right track and to focus more resolutely on the importance of that first year of development.

FOCUS ON THE FIRST YEAR.

Birth to three months – what to do…

- Talk to your baby as you walk around and introduce them to the world around them in their home. Listening to your voice will help your infant with the rhythm of speech. Sing songs and nursery rhymes at this stage too. Make eye contact and try out some little actions while you are spending time together.

Three to six months – what to do…

- Extend baby's reach by putting safe toys just out of reach so the baby must try to stretch and grab them. Put your baby on the floor or a mat on their tummy with the toys just in front of them. This is helpful for hand-eye coordination and the beginning of independent movement.
- Hold your baby in your arms and practice dancing as you move around the room with your baby, they will be enjoying movement with you.

Six to nine months – what to do…

This is a time to prepare for some mobility. Your baby could be sitting and trying to get moving. During these next three months your baby may start crawling or even standing and walking round holding onto furniture.

- Play some peek a boo games. Hiding behind furniture or around the corner and peeping out so your baby tries to find you. This game usually brings squeals of delight from your baby, but at the same time it is developing what is known as object permanence. That is the concept of knowing something is there even if it is not seen for a moment.
- Climbing cushions. Pile up some cushions from the lounge furniture and encourage your baby to climb the cushions. This requires supervision of course but it will help your baby with balance and climbing motions.
- Copycat. Copy each other actions. Soon your baby will get the idea and you can have a lot of fun imitating each other. It teaches your baby about learning through imitation.

Nine to twelve months – What to do….

- Take reading books more seriously. Pointing to pictures and repeating vocabulary or making sounds to go with the pictures is a great way to develop language. Find board books with thick board like pages to turn and let your baby turn the pages of the book.
- Sound imitation can continue with just copying the noises

your child makes. Have fun making silly noises to each other. These are all the building blocks of learning language.
- Water play is important at this stage. Bath time can be a great learning experience with pouring and measuring. Include lots of water play toys for bath time.

Encouraging activities in the next year of your child's life will engage you in the early stages of a toddler. Your little one will finally take their first steps, and this will be a big game changer for you and the family.

YEAR TWO AND HOW TO STIMULATE YOUR TODDLER FOR BRAIN DEVELOPMENT:

A year of reaching more and more physical and mental milestones. Your little one is entering the toddler phase. Character is starting to develop, and this phase is often known as the terrible twos as your toddler begins to be assertive. No is a very popular word.

Movement skills are developing at a rapid rate. Your toddler should be trying to:

- Start to run.
- Kick a ball.
- Carry several toys at one time.
- Climb up and down from the furniture.
- Hold on and walk up some stairs.
- Throw a ball overhand.

- Walking has become more stable and they may be able to walk backwards or stand on one leg.
- All their movements are becoming more coordinated.

Encourage running, climbing, sliding, and exploring outside. All under supervision at this stage. Remember that movement stimulates the brain and fine motor skills are beginning to develop as your two-year-old should be able to move their wrists, fingers, and engage the palm of their hand on a knob or handle. They can grab a crayon and scribble with it although the lines are very uncoordinated. You may start to see a left- or right-hand dominance but there is no need to force them to choose at this stage. They can concentrate for a little longer and will manage to turn the pages of a book with you.

Toddler language skills are developing rapidly as well. You may start to notice these developments at this stage.

- Knowing the names of their siblings, some of their body parts and objects they see often.
- They can follow simple instructions.
- They point to pictures in books and can name some of them.
- They are trying to string words together into little sentences.
- They repeat words they hear others say.
- They are using some pronouns like me and I instead of using their names.

Books are your best friend for developing language and saying the names of everything you see in the pictures. Remember, while out and about with your toddler you can be pointing out interesting things to see and find out about. They will enjoy rhymes and songs too but don't worry if your toddler is not speaking as much as another toddler you know. Language development is very different for each and every child growing up.

Social and emotional skills are developing at this age and your toddler should get excited about being with other children. They will play beside other children in what is known as parallel play and will be starting to become more independent. The toddler trend of being defiant will be showing through as their character develops and they are more aware of what they want.

The two-year-old is developing their thinking skills and here are some things to encourage.

- Sorting by shape and color. Shape posting games are very good for the simple coordination of fitting the shape into the correctly shaped hole in the toy.
- Learning to follow a two-part instruction like – fetch your hat and put it on your head.
- Finish the end of rhyme they know in a book from memory.
- They can enjoy simple make-believe games.
- They will start counting and understanding numbers.
- Their language skills are improving, and they can solve little problems or situations.
- They may begin to understand some concepts of time like before and after.

The more activities you can engage in to develop these milestones the better for your toddler. Some little ones may be going to a play school a few mornings a week depending on family circumstances and the child's emotional readiness. Some children may have to attend a care facility if their parents are having to work. In all circumstances it is important to make sure the facility is providing the right experiences for your child at the appropriate age group.

GET READY FOR YEAR THREE.

Here comes another year of exciting growth and challenges to meet. Knowing some of the expected milestones of development helps parents plan activities and know what to expect. Remember that each child is an individual and no milestone is cast in stone. However, if you do suspect your child is delayed in any aspect of their growth and development then getting professional advice is always a good idea.

Here are some of the expected milestones when your child reaches the age of three.

Physical development and improvement skills:

- Your toddler can jump and may be able to hop on one foot.
- Children at this age can climb and run confidently.
- Three-year-olds can pedal a tricycle.
- Your child should be able to walk up and down stairs one at a time.

Communication with others and language skills:

- Has started to make little sentences with a few words strung together.
- Speech has become clearer and even strangers to the family can understand what your child is saying.
- Can follow instructions with 2 – 3 things to do.
- Knows the names of some of their friends.
- Uses some pronouns like I, you, we and is starting to use simple plurals like dogs, cars, cups and so on.
- Has little 'conversations' beginning to interact with parents and friends.
- They are starting to use their imagination with their language skills.

Thinking skills and cognitive development:

- your three-year-old can turn the pages of a book that is age appropriate.
- They can stack up to six blocks to make a tower.
- At this age they know some of their colors.
- Their little fingers can manage 2 – 3-piece puzzles.
- They should know what two means.
- Three-year-olds start to draw and copy circles.
- They enjoy toys with buttons to press and levers to pull.
- Your three year is starting to enjoy fantasy play and make-believe stories with their toys and people they know.

Emotional and social skills:

- At this stage your toddler wants to dress and undress by themselves.
- They love to be helping and are ready to get involved in some household chores.
- The three-year-old likes to copy other children and adults.
- At this age your child may be potty trained.
- They are becoming more independent and do not get upset when their parents have to leave them at day care for example.
- The three-year-old is very affectionate and ready to show affection.
- They are concerned when friends are upset.
- The three-year-old is more likely to be persuaded to take turns with other children.
- The three-year-old enjoys having a routine and sticking to that routine.

Now that you know what to expect from the three-year-old phase here are 10 suggestions of things you can do as you go about your everyday life to encourage the developmental milestones at this age. Take note of these ideas and soon they will become a regular part of your everyday routine too.

1. Read a story every day. Bedtime is always a good time. Use this as an opportunity to develop language and ask a few

questions about the story or point out interesting things in the pictures.

2. Sing songs together and play little action rhymes too. If your child is at preschool, they will be learning rhymes and the actions to go with them.
3. Make sure your child has plenty of time to play. Fantasy play and active playtime are important. Put together a dress up box or basket with different things to encourage fantasy play.
4. Take time to arrange play dates and spend time with friends. Encourage sharing at this time. Put away any really special toys that would cause an incident but make sure there are lots of toys the children will happily share and take turns playing with.
5. Try some fine motor activities like coloring with big chunky crayons at first. Encourage play dough if you know your child will not want to put it in their mouth.
6. Have a structured routine bedtime and try to stick to it every day.
7. Help your child to understand and express their feelings. If they are sad or angry or happy talk about that feeling and the word to describe how they feel at that moment.
8. In our modern world screen time and technology is a relevant point of discussion. Keep screens out of the bedroom and monitor what your three-year-old watches. It must represent quality programs that are interactive where possible. Limit screen time to an hour a day and participate in the educational programs to avoid using the device as a babysitter.

9. Praise the behavior you want to see. Positive affirmation is very important to bring out the character traits you want in your child.
10. If you need to discipline your child use the incident as a teaching tool. Recommend 'time in' together to understand the incident and your boundaries of right and wrong behavior. 'Time in' is more effective than 'time out.'

The first three years have flown by and when you look back on how your child has grown in so many ways you will be amazed. The milestones they have accomplished and the development you have seen physically, mentally, emotionally, and socially have all been quite astonishing.

Now in these early formative years it is time to view the four- to five-year-old phase as a finishing line for the early years in a child's life.

WHAT TO EXPECT FROM YOUR CHILD IN YEAR FOUR AND FIVE.

One of the biggest developmental things you will notice is how much more independent your child has become. Four- to five-year-olds are more confident and have greater self-control. You will be seeing signs of development that stem from your positive parenting during the first three years. Some children may have a younger sibling and perhaps they are already at a more formal preschool. Their increased maturity and confidence help them to cope with these new additions and changes to their lifestyle. Cognitive and language development skills are growing in front of your very eyes. Socially your four- to five-year-old is far more manageable.

Here are some of the exciting milestones to look forward to at this age:

Fine and gross motor/movement.

- Running, climbing, swinging, hopping, and kicking or throwing a ball easily, is what your four- to five-year-old should be doing on the gross motor side of their development.
- They should be able to hop on one foot.
- Pedal a tricycle.
- Walk backwards and forwards.
- Build a tower with ten blocks.
- Use a fork and a spoon to eat with.
- Dress and undress, brush their teeth and manage other personal grooming needs without too much help.
- They should be able to draw a person with a body.
- Their drawing should include copying shapes like a triangle, square or circle.

Cognitive and language skills at this stage:

- You should notice how curious your child is about the world around them.
- They are chatty little people who have a growing vocabulary.
- This age group enjoy singing songs and remembering

rhymes. They are chatty and can be funny, energetic, and noisy.
- They can count up to ten or more objects, recognize four or more colors and three shapes.
- The four- to five-year-old will be wanting to write their name and may know a few letters in the alphabet.
- You can see a definite development to their span of concentration.
- They should know their address and phone number.

Social and emotional development:

- the four- to five-year-old enjoys playing with their friends and making them happy.
- They are beginning to realize the world does not revolve around them.
- At this stage of development, they are beginning to understand games have some rules and they have to take turns.
- The four- and five-year-old is beginning to say how they feel and can express their anger.
- Most children at this age are fitting in happily into a school routine but still need plenty of time to play and have the freedom to create their own fantasy games and have free playtime.

If you as a parent have any concerns over your child's development at this stage of their growth it would be a good idea to take them to see a specialist for a second opinion or a professional viewpoint. Perhaps your child's teacher has mentioned a few problems at school, or you have noticed your child has some delays or emotional issues. The earlier these are defined and dealt with the better.

Here are some points to look for and have investigated if you are concerned.

- Is your child very anxious about being away from either of their parents?
- Does your child find it difficult to concentrate on a task or game?
- Do you notice your child does not make eye contact with other adults or children?
- Your child is not able to build with blocks and balance them to make a tower.
- Is your child unusually sad or crying often and seems to be very miserable?
- Can you child say their own name?
- Does your child have difficulty dressing or brushing their teeth and is it difficult for them to use the bathroom?
- Do you feel your child is not happy in the company of other children?

If you answered yes to any of these questions it may be advisable to speak to someone about possible developmental delays. The key to success in the early years is to be actively seeking advice, information, and education through knowledge of the transformation children go through at this critical learning period of their lives.

The early years offer the child the greatest opportunities for physical, mental, emotional, and social growth. These four quotes from an educator, a psychologist, a theoretical physicist and an author of motivational books share some different ideas on the basic principles of child development.

Maria Montessori – educator and developer of the Montessori philosophy of education said:

> "Children acquire knowledge through experience in the environment."

She also said,

> "Education must begin at birth."

Jean Piaget, a Swiss psychologist was known for his work on child development and his theory of cognitive development and he said:

> "Play is the work of the child."

Albert Einstein, a theoretical physicist and one of the greatest minds of all time, said:

"Imagination is everything!"

— ALBERT EINSTEIN

Stephen Covey, American educator, author and motivational speaker said:

"Your most important work is ahead of you, not behind you."

— STEPHEN COVEY

This quote along with the others leads parents towards the future with their children. Guiding children through play to use their imagination and environment as the true tools of knowledge and growth. The early years of parenting are the most important years of all-round development and education through the power of play.

5

EMOTIONAL INTELLIGENCE

Emotional intelligence? Let's start this chapter with a description of emotional intelligence and why is it so important when considering child development.

Emotional intelligence or EQ, emotional quotient, is the ability to understand and manage your emotions in different ways to have positive outcomes. Emotional intelligence can help relieve stress, empathize with others, communicate, overcome conflict and create social awareness.

There are four types of emotional intelligence and they are divided into the following categories:

- Awareness of self.
- Management of your own person.
- Management of other relationships

- Social awareness.

How do we slot emotional intelligence into our balance of parenting and child development? It is like the fore and aft concept in terms of the yin and yang concepts of balance. The fore or the person with EQ is a leader and has leadership qualities while those who have not developed strengths in EQ may well be following the path set by the leaders in their community. This is equally as good as the leadership qualities because loyal followers are important in society too. The followers learn what the EQ is all about as they become the aft effect in the team. They are the backup heroes, the work ethic that the leaders need.

Being aware of yourself is the starting point for emotional intelligence. Knowing who you are and how you connect with others makes you so much more in tune with yourself. Using self-awareness gives you the ability to recognize other's emotions and how to react to them.

Managing yourself is the second aspect of emotional intelligence. It requires some self-control as you manage your own feelings in different situations. It is not about suppressing emotions but about recognizing them and managing them comfortably.

Management of other relationships. This involves being able to connect with others and build relationships away from your home group. Management of others is a skill built through making friends and getting to know other levels of emotional intelligence.

Social awareness brings into play the way you can understand others in different social situations. Having social awareness is an important part of making your life manageable in other social situations away from home.

Will your child learn to be the fore or the aft of the emotional intelligent relationship? Both have their place in relationships and the place may change from time to time as your child matures.

Back in the days of heroes who sailed the treacherous seas for their country, Horatio Nelson a famous British naval captain, had this to say about bravery at sea.

"Aft the more honor, forward the better man."

— HORATIO NELSON

This well-known saying has come to symbolize bravery and standing for your beliefs.

Nurturing emotional intelligence helps to create leadership qualities and to help followers know how to play their part in society. Leaders can lead and followers can follow and become leaders as they understand the function of emotional intelligence.

What qualities show that a child would have emotional intelligence potential? When you have found those qualities how would parents and care givers build on these qualities as the child matures? These are valid questions parents may ask.

The concept of emotional intelligence does seem somewhat abstract. Looking at some of the points that make up the degree of emotional intelligence in an individual, will help to recognize this form of intelligence and find how to build onto this part of a child's character. Emotional intelligence is of great worth in society, the home, and work environments.

Look at these 10 qualities defining Emotional intelligence. Do you see any of them in your children? These qualities show your child already has some degree of emotional intelligence. When you have identified them, you can build on them and encourage your child to grow in these areas as they face more social challenges.

1. Making emotional connections:

Do you see your child beginning to think about how others feel? It may come with a hug for a friend or a connection with you and the family at home. Your child may show empathy with a character in a storybook. These are signs of making an emotional connection.

How to encourage emotional connections:

- Spend more time with your child to foster emotional connection. It takes time and effort to form these connections. Your child sees how you do this through bonding with you.
- Be part of your child's world and play their games. When

you play with your child you can enter their world and talk about emotional connection on their level.
- Listen to your child's feelings and encourage them to talk about how they feel. Getting in touch with your own feelings helps you understand the feelings of others.

2. Thinking skills:

Are you aware of your child taking a moment to think about others or take the time to think about what they are going to do? Problem solving and thinking before acting is a sign of emotional intelligence.

How to encourage taking time to think about others.

- When you see your child being kind in any situation commend them for their act of kindness.
- Talk about caring gestures. How do we show kindness to others is a good topic of conversation.
- Be a good role model yourself. Let your child see how you show kindness in your family and to others.
- Talk about how to speak in a way that shows you are a thoughtful person.

3. Accepting criticism:

There may be times when you have to tell your child you did not like their behavior and why. How do they accept the comments you make? Do they show a desire to learn and do things better next time, or are they angry at the way you spoke to them?

How to show your child to accept criticism.

- Be sure to tell your child you are criticizing the action and not being negative about the child.
- Help them to understand that pointing out faults helps people to grow into better people. It is meant to be helpful.
- Be understanding in the situation and ask questions if you need to dig deeper and resolve the hurt feelings.

4. Showing empathy:

Genuine empathy takes time to develop and this is a characteristic you would be working on as a parent. How is that going? Do you feel your child is responding to your encouragement of empathy?

How to help your child show empathy.

- Talk about the feelings others may have. Books are a great introduction to feelings and sharing feelings.
- Be a good example of empathy and talk about how your child felt when you showed you wanted to understand their feelings.
- Use pretend play with your child's toys to create a situation where a toy shows empathy towards another toy. Use the dialogue of this situation to bring out the empathetic response from your child.

5. Saying sorry:

Being humble and saying sorry is something parents should be teaching their children. When they are knowingly in the wrong, they should show remorse and say sorry.

How to show your child to say sorry with meaning.

- Help children make the connection between what hurts if they have upset another child, and what they are saying sorry for.
- Instead of just saying sorry say I am sorry for....
- Let your own actions speak about being sorry by demonstrating how sorry you are. Your child will follow your lead.

6. A child who keeps their promises shows emotional intelligence:

Children can make promises and not keep them as they dash off in other directions and forget what they said. A child who keeps promises and remembers their commitment is showing they are going to have emotional intelligence.

How to be a good role model to show your child the value of keeping promises.

- First and foremost, parents need to be a good role model when it comes to keeping promises.
- Talk about how to make promises that can be kept. Don't

promise something beyond your reach because you are setting yourself up for failure and disappointment.
- Help your child have a plan to reach the goal of the promise they want to keep. A promise that is attainable through some simple steps.

7. Being helpful:

Children who are naturally helpful and like doing things for others are definitely blessed with emotional intelligence. When they want to help others, they are showing they have empathy and kindness and an emotional understanding of how another person feels.

What you can do to encourage helpfulness.

- Find age-appropriate things to do where your child can help.
- Praise their helpfulness.
- Show how helpfulness bonds your family and builds your friendships.

8. Saying kind words:

Children who speak kindly of their friends and family members have the ability to praise others. This is part of building a trust between friends and family members.

How to teach children to say kind words.

- Help your child understand what kind words are and how they make people feel when you say them.

- Practice saying kind words at the supper table. When it is time for the family to be together and have a meal make this a time for sharing kind words.
- Start learning kind words with just a few words and build up your repertoire.

9. Forgiving another child for a wrongdoing.

At a young age children are more likely to forgive and forget, but as they mature and have better memories this may be something they need to work on to develop emotional intelligence.

How to help your child understand forgiveness.

- Talk to your child about forgiveness and how it means letting go of anger or bad attitude towards someone.
- Tell them to forgive takes courage and find some books about forgiveness.
- Think of real-life situations when you or your child have had to show forgiveness.
- Young children need to know about loving and caring for others before they can forgive.

10. Giving credit to others.

Children can learn from a young age to give high fives and clap hands to show praise for something another child has done well. You will soon see if your child is really giving praise because they want to boost another child. This is quite an advanced concept for the younger egocentric toddlers. Show how it works and they will soon catch on.

How to show your child the value of giving credit where credit is due.

- Start by showing your child how you value them. Give your child credit with words of affirmation.
- Uses thumbs up or high five signs to show immediate positivity for something they have done.
- Have a credit chart at home and add daily credits that are due for different things. Have the whole family on the chart and show your child how to award credits for other members of the family.

The ten situations listed here are different opportunities to show your child aspects of emotional intelligence. While you are being a good role model in these areas you are able to see how they respond and coach them in the different aspects of emotional intelligence.

One of the most successful ways to help children build emotional intelligence is through being a role model and coaching your child through setting the right example. Put empathy, kindness, forgiveness, and helpfulness into your daily living.

As your child grows and becomes part of other communities add those qualities into the different aspects of their life. Help them to be emotionally aware of their friends at school or their relatives at family functions. Make a point of spreading positivity everywhere and acknowledging it at every opportunity.

> *"I've learned that people will*
>
> *Forget what you said, People will*
>
> *Forget what you did, but*
>
> *People will never forget how*
>
> *You made them feel."*
>
> — MAYA ANGELOU

Teaching children to develop emotional intelligence is an enriching life skill and one they will all benefit from as they begin to see those qualities in you their parents and themselves as they grow older.

6

ROLE MODELS TO LOOK UP TO

Great role models come and go depending on the situation you are in. In every walk of life there are role models. Parents need to be their children's first role models. In the yin and yang of balance in nature and in our homes, parents are the best role models bringing both male and female roles to the family dynamics.

WHY YOUR CHILD NEEDS ROLE MODELS TO LOOK UP TO.

A good role model helps a child try to become the best they can be through imitation of good virtues and qualities. It is often easier for a child to see the qualities of good character being acted out in front of them than constantly being lectured on how to be a better person.

Role modeling is not about being the perfect person. It is about displaying honest, stable characteristics that help the character growth of another person.

Here are seven-character traits that are often spoken about in connection with a good role model. Read through this list and see if they are role model traits you feel are important in positive parenting.

1. A role model shows they respect others and are concerned for their well-being.
2. A role model has a sound knowledge of their subject and is open to learning new things.
3. A role model is willing to learn and accepts that they make mistakes.
4. A role model is a good communicator. They listen well and respond with meaningful replies.
5. A good role model is not afraid to be different and proud of who they are.
6. A good role model is a confident person. They are positive and a calming influence.
7. A good role model goes out of their way to make others into better people.

Good role models inspire people to want to do their best. You should look at a role model and think 'I want to be like that.' The early learning phase of a child's life is exactly the time positive parenting can be shown as the role model in so many ways.

How parents role model in their homes is an important factor in raising children in a positive environment. Here are some of the key areas where good role modeling and good parenting go hand in hand.

Maintaining a healthy lifestyle.

Parents who show their children a healthy standard of living are helping towards healthy lifestyle choices for their children. A healthy diet, spending time on exercise and outdoor activities and good sleep patterns are among the most important lifestyle areas. It is in these areas that parents can set a good example for their children.

Treating everyone with kindness and respect.

Parents need to show their children that everyone deserves to be treated with respect. This is a good quality to model at home and in the outside environment. Show your children that you treat everyone the same way including them. A great way of showing this is through the way you speak to others. Speak in the same tone of voice and do not make critical loud accusing kind of comments. Don't speak ill of others and gossip in front of your children. Even little ears can pick up on the fact that you are not being kind.

Good role models will show they have a love of learning.

Let your children see you enjoy books, hobbies, sports, music, visiting interesting places and trying new things. This helps to arouse a natural curiosity.

After mom and dad, children can see role models in their older siblings. They may just look up to them because they are older. Parents have to step in here and make sure their older children are being respectful of the family values and will act as a good role model. While they were raising the older sibling, the parents would have been encouraging the values they felt were worthy of being family values. An older sibling in the family should have the same values to impart with the younger members. Having family time when these values can be shared helps to bring about respect for role models in the family.

ROLE MODELS ARE A FORM OF MOTIVATION.

When you have someone to look up to, and you trust that person because you respect them, it is like having a 'picture' to copy. This is motivational for young children. They have a way of knowing what makes them feel good before they can put words to the behavior. Praising every step of the way for the good behavior is how to show your appreciation for the role model.

There are other intentional role modeling qualities parents and care givers would want their children to see. Intentionally sharing these qualities help young children to grow in the right direction.

Praise these qualities as you see them with your children.

- Dependability
- Compassion
- Integrity
- Honesty
- Connecting with others.

These are righteous qualities and when parents have an opportunity, they should compliment their children on showing these qualities towards each other and in front of their friends.

Think of ways to create opportunities for your child to see these qualities role modeled by yourself or others. Here are some examples of each of these qualities.

Dependability:

You always remember to pack sandwiches and something to drink for your child to take to school. When you coach them to say thank you, you can share with them how you do this every day, and they can depend on you when they open their lunch box at break time.

Compassion:

A family member is not feeling well or is feeling sad and lonely. You take your child with you for a visit to cheer the person up. You speak kindly to the person, perhaps it is your mom, or another family member and you show compassion. After the visit you explain to your child what you did and how it made someone else feel. Perhaps you included your child in the cheering up process by getting them to make a well wishers card.

Integrity:

This is a difficult one for young children to follow. It is about having strong ethics and morals and treating people with honesty and truthfulness. The best way to encourage integrity is to praise the good you see in your child. Look for those 'good moments' and praise them. This kind of positive praise will influence the way your child sees how some actions taken by others can make their friends happy or sad. The way you deal with your child is evidence of your integrity as well. Always treating everyone the same way shows integrity.

Honesty:

This is very important for young children. Apply honesty to everything. Don't lie about treats or time with your child. Don't give them false hope of a new toy or time out with you when you know it is not going to happen. Dishonesty builds lack of trust and this is not a good style of role modeling.

Children will soon see if you are really dedicated to an activity. If you are organized, on time and committed they can follow your lead on being dedicated to an activity. If it is something they can join in with you then take them along and let them appreciate what goes into making this activity successful.

Another great way to use role modeling to good advantage is to look for characters in story books. Read the stories and point out the good character traits that the heroes and heroines are showing through the story. There are books about kindness and empathy beautifully illustrated and the pictures make good talking points too.

Books can cover different cultures and acceptance of different traditions around the world. Books can illustrate courage and bravery while the characters are still children. When your child is more mature books with real life characters from the past can share stories of heroes from history and brave men and women who have made their mark on our society today. All these stories about great men and women are powerful tools to share how role models can improve the way we learn how to live.

Role models appear on TV shows and even animated cartoon characters can be role models. The popular dinosaur Barnie has great encouraging messages for young children. Puppet shows are appealing to young children and the Muppet characters are unlikely heroes, but they are full of character and funny too. When you read a story or watch a program on TV take time to point out the qualities you think are role modeled by the performers on the show. Ask your children why they liked a particular character and see if they are beginning to pick up good qualities that they would like to copy.

Positive role modeling at preschool.

A well-run preschool is the perfect environment for creating role model situations. The teachers need to be alert to the character traits they wish to copy and to pass on to others.

Here are some of the character traits a preschool likes to pass on to its pupils by making examples of children who are showing these quality characteristics.

Polite behavior and good manners.

Preschoolers are encouraged to act in a polite manner thanking people for what they have done for them. It is also good manners to say please in situations that they want to have something done for them.

Sharing.

'Sharing is caring' is a phrase that has become synonymous with the preschooler. This is a good character trait to encourage as preschoolers find it difficult to share their toys and other possessions. They go through a very egocentric time in their lives and sharing is not on their agenda! Learning to share at preschool is the perfect place to look at role models for this activity. Everyone is expected to share, there is no feeling of being made to stand out in the crowd. If you do share something the accolades are there for you and everyone respects the role model who is sharing.

Social behavior.

At preschool children find themselves having to mix with other children. The teacher will highlight the behavior that is condoned by the age group and suggested by the teacher. Trained teachers will know what behavior is appropriate for each age group.

Honesty.

'Honesty is the best policy' is a good saying to remember. Watch out for little lies or hiding the truth. Teachers will be very aware of this situation and if your child does not tell the truth at school there will be consequences. Careful instruction to all the children will follow an incident of not telling the truth to teach little ones about the importance of being truthful.

Connecting with others:

Preschool is the ideal way to connect children with others. Through the school children will make friends and be invited on play dates. The staff at the school will be well aware of how to help children to connect with each other.

Role models in society.

When you are out and about in your community there are many opportunities to show children good role models. Point out the people who help us like nurses, doctors and the police officers. What qualities do these hard-working community orientated people share? Tell children how they serve others and what good role models they are. Once you are intentional about looking at role models you will see many opportunities to tell your child about good qualities and how other people help us every day.

Lead by example is probably one of the most important ways to show your children clearly the qualities you value and how they can trust in you while they are still young. People who lead by example keep their promises, know how to resolve difficulties and are mindful of others. Martin Luther King is always upheld as an inspirational leader. He modeled his strategies on the non-violent success of Mahatma Gandhi and won a Nobel Peace Prize. Martin Luther King's famous words said:

> *"I have a dream that my four little children will one day live in a nation where they will not be judged by the color of their skin but by the content of their character. I have a dream today."*
>
> — MARTIN LUTHER KING

Parents who have a dream for their children will want to base that dream on a solid foundation of positive parenting.

7

CALM RESPONSES IN ALL SITUATIONS

Keeping calm is a highly recommended parenting strategy. The 'Keep Calm' mantra has been attached to hundreds of different situations and occasions. It is seen on tea towels, framed on bedroom walls and adorning coffee mugs. In fact, the keep calm slogan, originally meant to help Britain face an eminent world war, has become one of the most famous sayings. Here are some examples of keep calm slogans.

- Keep calm and dance because you own the night.
- Keep calm and go sing in the rain.
- Keep calm and take one step at a time.
- Keep calm and drink your coffee.
- Keep calm and never give up.

Winston Churchill would probably have been proud of the last one.

Keep calm and never give up. There may be times in your parenting journey that you really do want to give up. Parenting is not for the faint-hearted. There will be many times when you are tested, and emergency situations will always be one of those times.

L R Knost author of 'Two Thousand Kisses a Day.' said:

"When little people are overwhelmed by big emotions, it's our job to share our calm, not join their chaos."

— L R KNOST

This can be a challenging thing to do in an emergency. Here are some tips and suggestions for how to react in a challenging situation.

1. Help your child to stay calm by being calm yourself

This may seem like a very difficult thing to do, but as the adult and the parent in whatever situation you find yourself in, being calm yourself will definitely help your child remain calm too.

2. Practice calming down strategies with your child

Teach your child deep breathing and speaking in a calm voice. Learn to connect with a gentle hand touch. Spread the palm of your hand and fingers open and gently touch palms with your child. Not a great big slap high five generated motion but a quiet connection that is reassuring. From this calm but firming position you can talk directly to the child and reassure them with calm words of your own. This is assuming the situation is not an emergency situation.

3. Find coping skills to manage different kinds of stress

Stress may come in different ways and therefore be made known in different situations too. Finding the right coping skills is helped by getting in touch with your feelings. Encourage your child to know what they are feeling and then find the right coping skill.

Here are some suggestions:

- Anger – deep breathing.
- Sadness – cry some sad tears and be comforted.
- Confusion – ask for help.
- Frustration – take what is frustrating you to solve the problem.

Every feeling that we have can have a positive outcome. Help children to identify the feeling that is making them upset. This may be difficult with the younger children who do not have the vocabulary to express emotions. They are probably just frustrated most of the time. Distraction is a good tactic until they can be more fully aware of their feelings and how to express them.

4. Have some problem solving strategies

Teach your child about problem solving strategies. What do they do in different situations and who do they go to for help. Always help your child to understand that keeping calm is the best way to handle a stressful situation.

5. Practice deep breathing

Deep breathing is simply a great way to relax because it sends messages to your brain telling the brain you are calm and relaxed. Deep breathing affects the nervous system and physically calms down your whole body. The more you practice this skill the better you will become at doing it. Teach your children to respond to a difficult situation with deep breathing too.

Now you have five strategies that will help in a generalized difficult situation, but as every parent knows difficult situations can be more challenging in some circumstances and need different reactions. Emergency medical situations will not necessarily respond to gentle hand connections for example. In very difficult life-threatening situations, the response to the emergency would still be calm. Keeping calm and not giving up is a way of managing the emergency. Here are some home emergencies to look at and the approaches to managing in a life-threatening situation.

Here are some strategies to use to be prepared for a more challenging home emergency:

- Have your emergency numbers readily available. On your phone is a good idea. Put them on your contacts list under emergency or even as A for accidents. In this way you get the important numbers immediately.
- Call 911 if it is an emergency you cannot manage without professional help.
- Keep your car ready for an emergency if you should need to

rush to a doctor's surgery or an emergency room at the hospital.
- Have a home first aid kit and know how to use it if necessary.
- Have a neighbor or family member you can contact if you need to go to the hospital in a hurry. You can phone this person and they will be there to help.
- Know how to deal with a small fire like a pot of the stove. It is not by throwing water everywhere. A thick blanket of even a fire blanket is best.
- If your child has been burnt be ready to deal with the trauma and get to the doctor's surgery or hospital as quickly as possible or call an ambulance if the situation is really serious and you can't deal with it yourself.
- Have torches and battery-operated lights in case your emergency includes a power outage.
- Assess the situation and make the person or child comfortable as you reassure them help is coming. Loosen tight clothing so they can breathe and feel comfortable.

AND keep calm.

What should you have in your emergency first aid kit?

A well-organized first aid kit kept in a safe out of reach from children space is a very important set of supplies to have in your home. Having a kit like this will help you feel calm in different situations. The following items are recommended for your basic first aid kit.

- Disposable sterile gloves.
- Scissors.
- Tweezers.
- Plasters in different sizes.
- Triangular bandages
- Crepe rolled bandages.
- Sticky tape.
- Sterile eye dressings, at least two.
- Thermometer, digital if possible.
- Cream to deal with skin rashes.
- Antiseptic cream.
- Antihistamine cream.
- Eye wash and eye bath.
- Pain killers like paracetamol for infants or children. Aspirin, not for children under 16, and ibuprofen.
- Monitor all medicines with absolute care and keep them out of the reach of little ones.

Prevention is better than a cure they say. What measures can you take as a parent to ensure the safety of your toddler at home. When you are sure your child is safe you will really feel calmer and in control of safety and security.

Toddlers are going through a time in their lives when they are curious and exploring everything. They are walking, running, climbing, jumping, and most of all learning about the world around them. You need to have the peace of mind that comes with knowing they are safe. They need to be supervised within the safe play area they have and you need to be able to supervise and see them at play.

Here is how you can feel that calm state of mind knowing your toddler is safe and still allow your toddler to have some freedom. Follow these guidelines to achieve the calm state you wish to have with your active toddler.

- Create a safe play space. This may require moving some pieces of furniture, but it will be worth it for the time that your toddler is vulnerable and needs a controlled space to play in.
- Stay nearby so you can hear changes in the noises made and always check if you suddenly cannot hear what your toddler is doing. Keep your eyes and ears open for a change in the background noises. When it comes to toddlers silence is not golden.
- Have a safety check list that applies to the area your toddler will be playing in. This will give you peace of mind and make you feel calm.
- Find out what safety devices are available to make your home safe and toddler friendly. Use security gates at the top and bottom of the stairs. Plug covers stop little fingers going into plug sockets and there are ways to lock and latch doors and windows. Safety locks in cars are another safety device.
- Check the cords hanging from blinds at the windows. Cords hanging loosely can be an issue with chocking an infant or strangulation. Keep cords at windows out of reach.
- Do not leave any household poisons or products that say 'Keep out of the reach of children' lying around. Young children tend to put everything into their mouths and a small

amount of a poisonous substance can do an enormous amount of damage to a small person.
- Check the temperature of your hot water. Boiling scalding hot water in a bathroom or the kitchen could lead to a terrible accident if a toddler decides to turn on the hot tap. Try to keep your hot water temperature at 120 degrees maximum.
- Never leave hot foods or boiled kettles in the kitchen just at the level of the curious toddler. A cord from a kettle could be a hazard if the toddler should pull on the cord.
- Be aware of the possibility of drowning in ponds or pools of water. Never leave a toddler alone around containers of water. Swimming pools should have a net or be in a fenced and gated area with a latched gate that cannot open easily. Ponds should be covered or out of reach of a toddler.
- Use a car safety seat for traveling with a toddler and make sure they are buckled in and secure on any journey. Long or short the car seatbelt is a very necessary security item.

If you have taken the right precautions, you will find the role of parenting and keeping calm is not so daunting after all. This phase does not last. Use the time as an opportunity to teach the basic rules of safety and remind your child that there are ways of doing things for safety's sake.

Toddler safety at home is relatively under your control, but what about taking your toddler out into the wide world. How will you keep calm while you and your toddler are out and about?

Here are four key areas to learn about keeping safe:

1. The car:

A car seat, safely installed in the car, is essential. There are safety regulations to follow and children under the age of two should have a rear facing seat. Never ever leave your child locked in a hot car. It is also important to keep your car locked at home and not allow children to play in a hot car. Keep car or kiddie locks on for safety so your child cannot get out of a car until you are ready to accompany them.

2. The car park and shopping area:

Going out shopping or visiting with a toddler can be a nightmare if you are not in control of the situation. Some parents will happily use walking reins with a harness to keep their child in check while they are out together. Children must learn to hold a parent's hand while they are out in a public place. This is a time where the safety rules are non-negotiable. Using a stroller with strapped in facilities will give parents more peace of mind and keep them in a calm state while they are out with their young children.

3. Sports and recreation times:

Bike helmets and safety gear are important when your child gets confident on a bicycle or even on a tricycle or scooter. Accidents happen easily in the playground. Check safety regulations on outdoor equipment and the age recommended for their use. Exercise and outdoor sports are very beneficial for young children but make sure that they are well supervised and age appropriate. When you are watching you want to feel confident that your child can manage the activity and you can feel calm as you enjoy seeing them participate.

4. Visiting friends:

Your home may be toddler friendly and safe, but your friends and family may not be at the stage of having a toddler running around. There are some things you can check and be reassured about before you visit.

Here are some essential points to consider for your peace of mind and feeling calm.

- Swimming pools. Are they safe and secured with a net or a fence and locked gate? Are there any other sources of water that could be a danger to a toddler or a child who cannot swim?
- Pets. Do your friends have pets and are they safe with children? If they are not sure about how their pet, especially a dog will react to a small child then ask your friend to put the dog away during your visit.
- Guns. This is something no one wants to talk about but if you think there is a possibility your friend or their partner has a gun for any reason then it is safe to ask where the guns are kept and ask if they are they safely locked up and there is no access to the guns.
- The bathroom can be a hazard if there are medicines that are not securely locked away. Toddlers love to explore so if you are not with them and they explore the bathroom and find

- medicines not locked away they will be sure to help themselves.
- Toys can be a hazard. Consider your toddler and the age of the other children. Small blocks and games like Lego can be a choking hazard.

One of the most challenging situations for a toddler's parent is keeping calm in the face of a temper tantrum. Although it may be difficult at the time the most important ingredient to the recipe for sorting out tantrums is to keep calm!

Then it is a good idea to try and have an understanding of why these tantrums can happen. One of the main reasons is children in this age group do not have the words to express how they feel. Tantrums help them to try and manage their feelings. Older children can have tantrums too, but these outbursts of emotion are mostly associated with the 'terrible twos'.

Here are four possible triggers for a tantrum to consider:

1. Stress.

When toddlers feel hungry, tired, out of routine, and over stimulated they can feel out of control. This kind of stress that they cannot manage to understand may well set off a tantrum.

2. Strong emotions.

When children feel strong emotions like worry, fear, anger or sadness they cannot handle these emotions and the only response they can have is to have a tantrum.

3. Temperament.

Children are wired differently. A highly sensitive or volatile child may react differently in some circumstance and this kind of temperament leads to a tantrum. You will know how your child's personality may set off a tantrum.

4. An unmanageable situation for a toddler.

Toddlers are still very little people. There may be circumstances that throw them into a situation they do not have the words or physical ability to cope with. Often it is because they want something but cannot explain what or why they need this particular item. The frustration of being in a situation they cannot control or understand sets off a tantrum reaction.

How should parents react to tantrums in order to keep calm in the situation and be reassuring?

These suggestions should help with the management of tantrums. The most important thing is to stay calm. It is not always easy in the circumstances but try to take a moment to calm yourself. Then….

- Remember why you are staying calm. Getting angry just makes the situation worse. Keep your voice calm and react in a composed manner.
- Once a tantrum has started it is best to try and wait as it passes as long as your child is not in danger. Don't try reasoning with your child once a full-blown tantrum is in progress.
- Take a moment to try and understand their feelings. When

you empathize with their feelings, they sense you are on their side and not in complete opposition.

- Try to take charge of the situation and react in a clam but deliberate fashion. Always be consistent in these tantrum moments. That means not giving in sometimes and then being super strict at other times.
- Have a plan of action to deal with tantrums. Putting a strategy together will help you to feel calm because you will know what you are going to do. Remember tantrums are not going to last.
- Keep a sense of humor but don't laugh at the tantrum because your child may see this as getting the attention they were looking for and the tantrum may just continue. Always deal with a tantrum calmly and with your plan in place.

How does one remain calm in challenging situations? The key to being clam is patience. While you are waiting for your toddler to calm down you will be drawing on your patience. One of the lessons learned through history is patience can bring about victory.

Edmund Burke, an Irish statesman, politician and philosopher, wrote:

"Our patience will achieve more than our force."

— EDMUND BURKE

With this philosophy in mind, keep calm and carry-on being patient.

PART II

8

BLOCKING OLD HABITS AND PREVENTING OUTBURSTS

Let go of the old and bring in the new.

Can old habits be changed? Yes, they can, but it takes effort and a change of heart towards the old habit, and finding a way to the new one.

The number one revolutionary way forward would be to identify and acknowledge the bad habit. Whatever it might be face it, acknowledge it, and make a plan to change it.

Bad habits have a way of stopping you from reaching your goals. In parenting, recognizing a bad habit, is going to make your parenting easier. You will lift the block of repeating something that does not work simply because you acknowledge it. Then you need to look for a way to change it and find a different path to follow.

First things first – what are some of the bad parenting habits you may have acquired? These habits could be from your parents, or they could be things you believe in that are not strictly true or perhaps you have seen your friends and associates parent in this way and so you have been following their lead. Finally, your own temperament and nature may be influencing how you are acting as a parent.

Here are some parenting mistakes that you may identify with and once you recognize them you will be able to change them or modify your parenting methods.

Bad Habit:

Not allowing your children to make a choice of their own.

Children need to get some opportunities to make decisions or choices. Choosing the clothes they want to wear or the spread they want on their toast are simple choices they can make. If you are too controlling, you will not allow your child to learn about independence and the wisdom of their own choices.

What to do:

Letting children make some of their own decisions gives them a sense of empowerment. Help your child with their planning and answering questions around their decision to do something in particular. This is your supporting role. You help them make an informed decision, but they have a sense of empowerment as they grapple with decision making.

Bad Habit:

Not really listening to your child.

Children know when you are not really paying attention to them. When you are listening be sure to be fully engaged with your child. In this way you get a better chance to understand through their body language, and what they are actually saying, how they may be feeling.

What to do:

Listening is about paying attention. You can hear your child as a million other things are going on but are you really listening to them. Real listening means you show with your body language and eye contact that you are tuned in and part of whatever your child has to say. Turn off any other distractions and aim for some one-on-one time with your child every day.

Bad Habit:

Being overprotective.

Some parents fall into the trap of wanting to pick up the pieces all the time. It is OK to let your child make a mistake and feel the consequences. Obviously, something that would cause bodily harm, or great emotional damage, it would not be wise to allow.

What to do:

Don't be afraid to let your child make small mistakes. Give them opportunities to explore with consequences that they can learn lessons from. Don't be over controlling by making all their choices for them including picking out their friends. Making choices is good for their maturity and developing a sense of personal responsibility.

Bad Habit:

Feeling guilty as a parent.

If you have had to say no, or if your child has to face a disappointment, you do not have to feel guilty every time this happens. Knowing how to deal with disappointment and not getting your own way is a life lesson children need to learn.

What to do:

Parents should have set a boundary that covers disappointment and helps children understand they don't get everything their own way. There should be no guilt attached to saying no to your child. We don't all get everything we want all the time.

Bad Habit:

Overreacting in difficult situations.

Don't jump to the highest degree of reaction when something out of the ordinary happens. Sometimes your child may scream out of the blue and you immediately go into flight and fright and freeze mode all bundled into one.

What to do:

Instead of overreacting take a moment to decide on how serious the problem is. A problem on the scale of 1 – 10. You will find that most of your worries are little ones.

Bad habit:

Keeping your emotions away from your children.

Many parents feel they cannot share their emotions with their children, and they keep their guard up and appear distant or angry during a crisis or even during some small irritation. They do not share their emotions.

What to do:

If you are angry say you are angry, if you are sad say you are sad. Help your children to get in touch with their feelings. Remember children deal with many of the same kinds of emotions that adults do. You can relate to these emotions too. Not everyone can be on cloud nine every moment of the day.

Bad Habit:

Being over critical.

Some parents are looking for perfection. Instead of finding something good to say they may just focus on the negative, or the why did you do that or not do the other, and finding negative things to say. Always picking out little details that were wrong takes away a child's self-confidence.

What to do:

Look for the good in every situation. Parents don't need to point out the wrong things all the time. Remember there is no harm in offering to help. Don't set your child up for failure. You can always step in and offer support instead of a critical comment.

Bad Habit:

Being inconsistent.

Parents need to set boundaries or house rules that are consistent.

When parents do not have boundaries, children feel insecure and will not have guidelines in place for their healthy growth and development.

What to do:

Set guidelines that are flexible. Taper your guidelines according to the age of the children, but nonetheless there does need to be some simple limits that define the child's behavior. You are consistent with your parenting based on these guidelines. Consistent parenting helps you to connect with your child on an emotional level that is positive.

Bad Habit:

Raising your voice when it is not necessary.

Parents who are always yelling or shouting at their children will not have effective communication and control over them ultimately. Yelling causes a vicious cycle of more yelling as children act out their bad behavior and parents yell even more. Yelling does not work.

What to do:

Start by not yelling about the small stuff. Make a conscious effort to speak in a normal voice for normal things at home. Recognize your 'trigger moments' and be ready for them. If getting ready for school and the breakfast routine is a trigger moment, then try to be ready beforehand so a simple thing at that time doesn't trigger a tirade of verbal abuse for something really manageable.

With these glaring mistakes in mind parents should try to see how they identify with each mistake. Find the one that stands out the most and try to break the habit and find another way of facing the problem. Look at this chart below. See the list of the old habits together with a new approach.

Compare an old habit with a way you can change to a new way of doing things.

Make a plan to change bad habits one habit at a time.

Bad Parenting Habits Revealed.	Reverse the Habit Here.
Not allowing your child to make choices.	Allow your child to decide on some things for themselves even if you don't approve.
Not listening when your child talks to you.	Pay more attention to what your child says and how they say it.
Being overprotective.	Let go in some situations to give your child the right amount of freedom.
Feeling guilty about your parenting.	Have boundaries and rules in place that benefit your child's development.
Overreacting in difficult situations.	Keep calm and react wisely.
Hiding your emotions from your children.	Share your feelings with your child when it is appropriate.
Being over critical of your child.	Measure achievements in a way that is always encouraging and not trying to push your child further every time.
Being inconsistent in the decisions you make.	Always make fair decisions based on your family values.
Raising your voice when it is not necessary.	

Knowing some of the basic bad, or negligent parenting styles, makes you wonder what to look for in children to see if they are perhaps finding it difficult to follow their parents' model of parenting.

Here are some signs to look for that may indicate there is some lack of positive and consistent parenting going on. Even if you find your child has fallen into the grips of some bad parenting it is never too late to change things for the mutual benefit of parents and the child.

SIGNS TO LOOK FOR TO INDICATE BAD PARENTING STYLES.

- Parents who deprive their children of affection and affirmation will have children who have lost self-esteem and confidence. They are deprived of emotional affection.
- Parents who criticize their children continually do not give their child a chance to develop their own personalities. Children who are subjected to criticism constantly fear being put down.
- Parents who make fun of their children in front of others make their child feel they are worthless and only good for mockery.
- Parents may make their children feel worthless and dismiss their sensitive feelings and emotions, making it more difficult for their child to be in touch with their feelings.
- Parents who use guilt or money to control their child's behavior do not bring out the best in their child. Controlling children in any way will not bring them up as responsible individuals.

Keep it simple – know how much instruction your child can take at each age……

9

DEEP CONNECTION, UNCONDITIONAL LOVE

Making a deep connection and sharing unconditional love is an incredible aspect of positive parenting and guilt free discipline. How deep is the love you have for your child? You will only be able to answer that question when you have experienced some tough times and been through the different stages of development with your child.

The moment your newborn baby is put into your arms is the moment you understand what unconditional love really is. It is a bond that forms between you and your child that has no limitations and no restrictions. Unconditional love is a way of communicating with your child to share your love for them on a long-term basis. It has its fuzzy warm moments, and yes, love does conquer all, but when it comes to raising your family there is more to unconditional love than fuzzy moments.

Here are some truths to remember about unconditional love.

- Unconditional love is a selfless love for another.
- It is a love that accepts and forgives.
- Unconditional love respects children for who they are.
- It is protective, nurturing, and caring.

Unconditional love is not:

- Warm fuzzy feelings although you may get them often.
- It is not giving in to every request because you can't say no.
- Unconditional love is not manipulating your children to create the kind of dependency on you that you want from them.
- It is not permissive allowing no consequences to actions, or positive disciplinary action, that teaches children as they grow.

Unconditional love allows deeper connections to be fostered with children and there are specific ways to do this. The beauty of unconditional love is it can be very forgiving and if mistakes are made unconditional love is there to overcome. Unconditional love changes in depth and input as you go through different phases with your child. Fortunately, love does grow because children have different needs at different ages and stages of their growth. A newborn for example will be needing more nurturing as their physical growth needs are met. A toddler will need the nurturing, but at the same time there will be a need to start with some discipline and learning through play. The preschooler will be needing to make choices and become more independent. The child who is in the early stages of primary school will need support with learning and getting organized.

Here are five simple acts of unconditional love using principles of positive parenting to apply to your child and help you be a supportive parent.

1. Say; 'I love you' often. Your child likes to hear they are loved.
2. Look for situations to give verbal affirmation.
3. Give loving touches of encouragement.
4. Spend one-on-one time with your child giving them individual attention and making them feel absolutely wonderful.
5. Show empathy towards your child by connecting on their level and trying to understand their feelings.

Now you are making great progress, but you want your connections to go further. Parents may find it gets more challenging as their children grow older to have a deeper connection. A connection that goes beyond the basic nurturing of an infant and a toddler.

What do you do to get this deeper connection and give unconditional love? You may be thinking right now that you are giving unconditionally to your child, but perhaps you are not sure of how this love can grow. What do you do beyond the cuddle and attend to physical needs time of your child's life? Your child is going to grow from helpless infant to wide awake contributing toddler in less than two years. The sooner you create that bond the sooner positive parenting can happen. As children grow and develop there are areas of child development that will always be enhanced through more unconditional love. Here are some other suggestions of ways to improve your love connection with your child through family activities and ways you can spend quality time together.

These suggestions will be helpful in the physical, emotional, and social areas of your child's development especially in the early years of growth. They are all ideas of simple ways to focus on unconditional love right there and then in your own home environment.

Keep the physical connection going.

Connect with your child through hugs, a pat on the back, an encouraging ruffle of their hair. All little gestures that just say, 'I'm here for you.' Share an evening cuddle while you read a story. Hug when you say goodbye and always make eye contact with a smile or a wave.

Play with your child.

This form of connection can't be emphasized enough. Play is the way young children learn and if you are right there learning through play with them you are forming a very strong bond. Share laughter together and high fives when you build a tower together or make a puzzle together.

Play outside and exercise together.

Running outside and kicking a ball together are great ways to connect. Show your love for your child by learning fun activities outside. Go to the local park or ride bikes together. Getting outdoors and exercising is a great unconditional love opportunity providing you do not impose too much competition on the activity.

Make your time quality time.

This time with your child should be uninterrupted time not half-hearted with part of you on the phone and part of you with your child. Make the time shorter if you are busy, but put the mobile phone away.

Create emotional connections.

When you acknowledge your child's feelings you help him/her to express those feelings. Keeping in touch with your feelings helps to create empathy and you and your child will have a stronger bond.

Strengthen your listening skills.

Ask yourself if you are really listening to what your child is saying or are you just hearing a background noise. Listen to what your child is saying not just through their words but by observing their body language too.

Use dinner time to interact with the whole family.

Sharing a meal together and having the opportunity to talk about their day is a great opportunity for children to get involved with their family. Encourage family meals sitting round the table.

Make the most of bedtime.

The end of the day with a bedtime story and last cuddles for the day is the perfect time to show your love for your child. You have a captive audience, and this is the ideal time to bring out some favorite stories and just look at books together. It won't matter if you read the same book over and over again. Children find comfort in the repetition.

Practicing unconditional love at home is probably easier than when you are out and about. Keeping emotionally connected to your child away from the safe haven of your home can be more challenging. How do you maintain this aura of unconditional love when you go out or when your child starts school? There may be times when you feel angry or frustrated but have a deep conviction about unconditional love and discipline will become more logical and a natural follow through on unconditional love. Remember discipline is part of loving your child through teaching them in different circumstances through discipline.

Outings can propose problems when your child is still young, and you are trying to teach safety rules and acceptable behavior.

How do you love unconditionally when you are angry?

Your toddler is being a typical terrible two and you are really cross with them. How do you manage to love unconditionally in these circumstances? Children need to know they are loved when they are being rather unlovable. It is easy to show your love and affection to your angelic child, but your child needs to know that love carries over to the angry, frustrated, and difficult moments too.

When your child is acting out their frustration or anger and disappointment it is time for you to help them get in touch with their feelings and to know that you still love the little person that they are, but you want to help them get past their feelings of anger or frustration.

Empathize with your child as much as possible. Share your own feelings too. When you are angry take some time to step back from the situation and calm yourself. If your child needs to learn a lesson from the incident, then take the time to guide and teach your child.

> *"Between stimulus and response there is a space. In that space lies out freedom and power to choose our response. In our response lies our growth and freedom"*
>
> — VIKTOR FRANKL

This famous quote from Viktor Frankl, Austrian psychiatrist, author and holocaust survivor, shows how between a stimulus that upsets you and your response to that stimulus is a space, a moment in time, when you can decide how you will react.

If you apply that philosophy to parenting and your reactions to different situations you will give yourself time to calm down and react differently. Your response could change dramatically in that space of time between stimulus causing upset and moment of response. Reacting in that way could make all the difference to your desire to give unconditional love.

In principle unconditional love may seem relatively easy. However, loving without reservation can be really trying at times. The backbone of unconditional love is not just a feeling, it is the ability to make your child feel loved exactly the way he/she is right at any given moment.

HOW DO YOU MAKE SURE YOU GIVE EVERYONE A SHARE OF THIS LOVE?

One of the wonderful aspects of unconditional love is that it does not disappear when the going gets tough. Unconditional love is always there to support and uplift the object of that love. Unconditional love offers freedom and support in equal measures and along with compassion there is really no limits to what unconditional love can give. Unconditional love tries to understand and connect with the other person in the relationship and this includes the child or children in the family.

10

BUILDING TRUST AND EMOTIONAL BONDS

Real trust takes time to build. It is not an overnight quick fix and parents have a defining role to play in helping children build trust in relationships.

Trust relies on a positive belief that there are good characteristics in people and in the world. Trust grows through positive affirmation starting at home. Adult interactions with children in and around the home are the first steps to building trust. The ability to build this trust is the foundation of positive parenting and parent/child relationships.

Your child's ability to trust you grows as you create a supportive environment for them. A strong foundation of trust makes an impact on a child's ability to have effective emotional and social connections with their world. This all starts with trusting in their parents. Although your child may not fully understand what trust is, you can start by using the word in conversations and attaching it to things you do with your child, and they do for you. When you ask your child to do something for you then say, 'I am trusting you will brush your teeth.' Or you may say 'I trust you enjoyed the story I read.' In this way your child associates the word and some kind of activity.

Trust is built when you keep your word. If you promise to fetch your child at a certain time your child trusts that you will do so. It is important that you do not break that trust by arriving late. Remember at this young age you are building trust and your child has no way of understanding that trust other than knowing you keep your word. Separation anxiety at this stage can be a very real thing as children have not developed a sense of time and place. If you say you will return in a few minutes or an hour you need to honor that time frame and build that trust with your child.

HOW TO BUILD TRUST.

There are ways to consciously build trust with your child from a young age. Putting the building blocks of trust in place will help you with many other values and principles you wish to establish for your family. Most of these suggestions are appropriate for all ages, but will need to be modified to suit the level of understanding your child has.

Building trust comes through being aware and intentional about these areas of your child's development. Here are some intentional ideas for the trust building aspect of your parenting.

Your word is key in all aspects of trust building.

Remember - *'Do what you say and say what you do,'*

This action helps children to associate keeping your word with following through with the actions you have said. When actions and words go together there is a huge association of trust. Words have more power than you think. Words show how much integrity you have. Children will soon pick up on the fact that you do not keep your word. The things you tell others including your children is what they come to believe about you. You need to be as good as your word. Your words should be a reflection of your character and by keeping your word you are seen in a positive light.

Be a good, non-judgmental listener.

A child who knows their parents are really interested in what they say will build a firm trust relationship with their parents. They will feel they are needed and that they are loved. Children need to know they can speak openly to their parents for a strong, trusting relationship to grow. Listening carefully is important for a number of reasons. Not paying attention can get you into trouble for a number of reasons and if you are not listening to your child you may become out of touch with their lives. Good listening puts you on a different level with your family. You can offer more empathy and intuition. A good way to become a better listener is to think about the difference between listening and hearing. Hearing is one of our five senses. When a sound goes into our ears it travels to the brain and in a very complicated process, we are able to hear. We hear sounds around us, music and of course voices. Listening on the other hand is a conscious action. We choose to listen. Listening is intentional and we can listen in different ways.

We listen practically to instructions and trying to understand things around us.

We listen socially trying to hear what someone is saying and understand what they are intending to say. We listen on this level with feeling and this type of social listening is often a head and heart affair. While we are listening, we treat the person speaking with respect.

We listen for personal development and give our attention to a speaker who is trying to tell us something for our edification or education. We treat people who we listen to for our personal development with regard for the knowledge or skills they can impart.

BEING A RELIABLE PARENT IS A BIG TRUST BUILDING ELEMENT OF PARENTING.

Children soon come to realize their parents make idle promises that they do not keep. They feel let down by parents and cannot depend on them. It is better to not make too many promises that cannot be kept. If you do promise to be at a certain place at a particular time you need to be there. Being reliable and dependable as a parent builds trust between you and your child.

The importance of building trust cannot be over emphasized. Trust enables parents to build on to other parenting and family values. The parent who is interested in their child on all levels of their growth will be able to encourage their trust as they show respect for their child's feelings and interest in the things their child enjoys.

What is emotional bonding?

Emotional bonding is the deeper knowledge of attachment a child has with its parents. It is the sense of feeling safe, comfortable, close to someone else, and happy in their company. It is an emotional connection, and without that connection, it is difficult to get close to someone. This is even more important while building connections with a child. Building this connection is not a 'once off' event. It is ongoing and as children get older, the trust needs to be greater. Sometimes you may break that trust and damage the bond. When you recognize you have done this then try as soon as possible to repair the damage.

How you may ask is that damage done? It can be as simple as not keeping your word. Perhaps it is forgetting something special in your child's life. Maybe it is a promise you were not able to keep. All your bond building relationships need attention from you to nurture them and grow your love bonding. However, if your bond is damaged it can be repaired.

How to repair damage from broken trust.

1. Set the wrongs right.

This will depend on what has happened in the past. If it is something small, then simply apologize and make amends through saying you are sorry and doing something together to build back the confidence your child had in you. If it is something more difficult set out some steps you plan to take to get back the close relationship you had. Tell your child you want to help them trust in you again.

2. Be understanding of your child's perception of the damage.

Take time to talk about what happened to break the trust. Try to be full of empathy to how your child felt. Did they feel let down, abandoned, mistreated, or neglected in any way. You will have to repair the negative feelings they have and take them into account as you move forward.

3. Ask for forgiveness.

This is important and children are generally forgiving. Find out exactly what it was that upset your child. Deal with that issue and ask for forgiveness for that particular act that you need to be forgiven for. Through seeking forgiveness your relationship with your child will grow as their trust in you strengthens.

One of the wonderful aspects of repairing the damage, and renewing the bond between parent and child, is your child is learning about how to say sorry with genuine intent. Genuine sorrow over some hurtful or unfulfilled promise leads to a deeper relationship. Forgiveness reignites the bond and strengthens parent and child relationships.

Sometimes a parent and child relationship may take on unhealthy proportions. How would you as a parent recognize that in your bond with your child? Emotional bonding that is too intense or dependent may not lead to the independent self-reliant child you hope to raise.

Here are some signs to look out for that may alert you to an unhealthy emotional bond.

Parenting style that is very controlling

Parents need to give their children their own space and let them make some of the decisions regarding their day-to-day activities.

Dictating the children's feelings and emotions

Parents who dictate how children feel do not allow them to understand and to express how they feel. Children need to know how feelings affect their lives and to be able to identify the way they feel at times of emotional experiences. Do they feel happy or sad, angry or frustrated and what does it feel like?

Keeping children in tight confined social boundaries

Parents who do not allow social interaction with other children are depriving their children of normal social interaction with their peers. Children need to meet and socialize with other children. Parents who keep their children in very controlled environments and monitor their every move are not raising well-adjusted children who are able to deal with different social and emotional situations.

Parents lacking in supervision with no discipline at all

The opposite of the controlling parent is the parent who has no interest in their child and the activities they are involved in. The child has no boundaries and no discipline. They are allowed total freedom with no parental supervision. This lack of control does not foster healthy bonds either.

It would be safe to say that parenting and forming healthy bonds with your child is an aspect of life that requires input on so many different levels. Forming a healthy bond however makes many other aspects of parenting easier to follow through and achieve the goals you have in mind.

This table may be helpful to see at a glance recognizable healthy bonding styles and their opposites.

Recognizable **unhealthy** bonding styles.	Bonding to build a **healthy** relationship.
Controlling children in every aspect of their day-to-day decisions. Choosing their clothing, their friends, their play routines and interests.	Allowing some freedom of choice within their home environment initially. Growing feelings of independence and responsibility.
Criticizing everything a child does as they try to take on more responsibility and are involved in more extra activities at home and in school.	Encouraging all efforts made in a positive manner. Always finding some good in a child's efforts whatever they maybe.
Creating an atmosphere of lack of trust through being unreliable or not placing importance on a child's place in the family or their needs.	Assuring children through words and deeds that they are important, and their needs and security are important.
Denying children of any real affection or affirmation that they are worthy and have a place of importance in the family.	Building children's self-esteem and confidence through loving gestures and words of affirmation telling them they are loved and needed.
Trying to create a miniature version of yourself through your child. You dress alike and act alike and transfer all your negative emotions trying to live through your child.	Children are individuals and not mini versions of their parents. Each child should be allowed to develop their own personalities.
Trying to be your child's best friend. Parents who want to be cool and on the same level as their children are not setting healthy boundaries.	Well-adjusted children should enjoy hanging out with their friends. Parents should allow them the freedom to spend time with their peer group.
Emotional manipulation is a way of getting what you want through making your child feel guilty or unnecessarily responsible for you and your happiness.	Children should be free to explore their own interests, make choices about their hobbies or sporting activities. They should be free to enjoy the company of others without their parents controlling their every move.
Having no boundaries. Allowing anything for peace and never saying no to your child.	Setting realistic boundaries to help your child with respect for other people in a relationship.

HOW TO START LETTING GO TO ENCOURAGE INDEPENDENCE.

Emotional bonding is essential in the early days of your child's growing and developing into a person. You take them through infancy with all the dependency they have on you. You nurture them as a toddler and help them learn life skills that prepare them for school. You guide them through primary school and beyond those difficult times. The end goal is to have a happy balanced individual who can lead their own lives. None of this independence will happen immediately but as you add in responsibilities and let go of some of the attachment your child should be learning to become independent.

Here are some steps to take from home to school to foster independence.

<u>Starting out with the toddler age group.</u>

Your toddler may be going to school because you are a working mom. You may have chosen to send your child to play school a few mornings a week to give them some social interaction. Whatever your motivation here are some tips to encourage your child to be ready for play school.

- Start by giving them some chores around the house. Helping you with dusting or putting toys and books away.
- Let them help you feed the animals if you have pets or water the garden.
- Find things they can do to help you and work at it together.
- Crossing the road may be an issue and if this is the case a set

of reins will help with control. You tell your toddler when they can listen and hold hands they can walk without the reins.
- Let them make some choices with you. Like the kind of sandwiches you are making or the flowers you want to pick. Listen to their choices you are just there to hear what they have to say.

When your child gets to primary school you will have taught them about being independent in some ways. Now how are you going to build that up?

- Ideally your school going child should be able to dress themselves and you should teach them to put on their own shoes and socks. Laces may still be a challenge, but children's shoes these days often do up with Velcro and that makes it easier.
- Your child should know how to use the toilet and wash their hands properly to be ready for school.
- Managing their own lunch box and wrappers to their food is another act of independence. Encourage them to make their own lunch at some stage.
- If your child did not attend a play school or spend any time away from home, make sure you have organized play dates and interaction with other children.
- Boost their self-esteem and confidence in little ways by encouraging them on the way to school and asking questions about their day.

SCREEN TIME AND ITS EFFECTS ON CHILD DEVELOPMENT

WHAT IS SCREEN TIME?

Any time that your child spends looking at a screen of any sort is classified as screen time. It could be a smart phone (yours) or a computer, an iPad or a television or video games. It is a time during your child's day when they are inactive, and they use very little physical energy during that time. It is estimated that many children spend around 3 hours a day watching and participating in some kind of screen time.

There are many questions surrounding screen time and many parents are concerned about the effect of screens on digital devices having a negative effect on their children. There are screen time guidelines, and these guides recommend children under the age of two are not exposed to screen time at all. Two to four hours was recommended for children over the age of two.

Here are some simple, easy, and effective ways to downsize the amount of television or screen time allowed in your home.

Do not have a television in your child's bedroom.

Studies into the effects of television in the bedroom have shown that TV in your bedroom results in disturbed sleep patterns. Access to TV in the bedroom leads to more time watching television over and above the recommended number of hours.

The negative effects are linked to the fact that the TV is taking the place of other things children should be doing at the end of the day.

Do not allow your child to eat in front of the Television.

Although the television makes a great spot to sit in front of and watch while you eat this is not the case for several reasons. Firstly, this way of eating prompts hunger triggers and lets overeating happen because you are more likely to eat more and exercise less. Eating in front of the TV leads to unhealthy snacking. The sound of the television lures the brain into thinking TV equals food and eating junk food leads to unhealthy living.

Try not to leave the TV on for background noise during the day or a family occasion.

Background TV is not good for children and it has been found that up to four hours a day may be spent in hearing background TV noise. What effect is this having on your children? Nothing you may think, it is just in the background. Well, it is not just background noise for a young child learning language. It is a disruptive noise that interferes with learning sounds to speak a language. Background TV has an impact on what the brain is able to do at a young age. This is why screen time and exposure to digital devices is NOT recommended for children under the age of two.

Do not allow children to watch TV while they do their homework.

This would seem like an obvious decision when children should be concentrating on their homework. However, in some homes the television is the center point of the home. It is flicked on at all times of the day. It would help to find a less public and more private place in the home for the television. The background noise is always going to be a distraction even if the picture is not visible. Having set watching times is a far better way of viewing and homework issues.

- Be a good role model and do not watch television all the time. Show your child that you are not addicted to the screen time. You have hobbies or you like to read or spend time in the garden, you do other things with your time.
- Keep a record of how much time your family spent on the Television and make a note of that time. Take the same amount of time for an exercise routine. Make use of this equation of time to go on an outing or visit the park but try to match time for time with something else other than screen time.
- Play other family games that do not involve looking at the screen of a computer or a television. Board games are a great

way of improving counting skills. Memory, and even general knowledge.

Today's children are growing up in a world of technology and parents are the generation of adults who have to try and determine how much screen time is suitable for their children. Digital devices provide hours of entertainment and educational material too. However, unlimited screen time can be harmful. There needs to be guidelines and boundaries. Children who are spending all day on digital devices are missing out on physical, mental, and social growth and development.

Here are some of the negative effects of too much screen time.

- Lack of exercise leads to obesity. Children who spend too much time sitting in front of a screen are not exercising and developing muscle mass and coordination skills. Movement and exercises are good for the brain too as it needs to be active to be able to develop certain concepts.
- Too much television, or having a screen in your child's bedroom, can cause sleep issues. Screen time just before bed is not a way to wind down. The blue light from the screen interferes with the sleep cycle of the brain and causes insomnia.
- Behavior problems can arise from too much screen time as children spend less time being sociable and interacting with other people or children.
- Violence in play activities can often stem from television programs of a violent nature. They affect children's interaction with others. Watching some violent programs

can leave a lasting impression on young children who will see these programs and want to act in a similar manner.
- Spending too much time on digital devices can be detrimental to family life. This applies to the adult as well as the child in the family circle.

Now that it has been established that screen time can be detrimental to your child's health it is important to look at how screen time can affect child development. Especially in the under three age group. A child who is exposed to too much screen time and watching the world go by in virtual reality is less likely to have time for playing, exercising, playing with friends and family, and being part of general family life. This can have a significant impact on their overall growth and development.

HOW DOES SCREEN TIME AFFECT CHILDREN'S MENTAL HEALTH?

This is a question on the lips of many parents. In our Yin and Yang concept of parenting on is the opposite of off. There should be a consciousness of what the outcomes are of having the on button engaged too much or the outcome of no interaction at all. The child who is not interacting with digital devices will grow up unable to function in a digital world. Everything in moderation always comes to mind. Parents who are informed are able to make the correct 'on or off' decisions and with that information choose the correct measure of screen time

Is a child's brain health affected parents may wonder. It seems that the answer to that question is yes, children's brain health may be affected This is the outcome of excessive screen time. Children were found to score lower on thinking and language tests. What has been found is that the electronic devices release dopamine, the brain chemical involved in cravings of satisfaction. Digital screen time is buying into this type of emotional hype.

Pediatricians have recommended the following guidelines for children with regard to screen times.

- **Children under 18 months** – should have no screen time.
- **Children 18 – 24 months** – could be watched with parents choosing high quality media programs.
- **Children from 2 – 5 years of age** - should be watching an hour a day. Some of this time should be spent with parents to check on the quality and content of the programs if possible.

The television should never be used as a baby-sitting tool. Language and literacy skills seem to be the most affected by too much screen time. Problem solving skills are compromised by too much screen time especially if parents are not selective over the quality of program being watched. Many of the children's programs, especially animated programs, do not have the quality of language parents would like their child to be learning. If everything is just about watching the animation, there is no real challenge to thinking or problem solving.

Research is ongoing into the pros and cons of screen time. It is fortunate that studies are being carried out as to the effects of screen time and while no definite decision has been made responsible parents would want to take a serious look at what screen time may be doing to their children. Screens cannot be banned. They are here to stay, the question is, how do parents deal with them.

An overall picture seems to suggest that very young children do not do well learning from screens. Older children can learn from screens, but the sedentary style of learning is not good for other aspects of their development. The effects of these devices are still being explored. In terms of a timeline did you know the first iPad was released on 3 April 2010? In terms of a timeline of inventions that is a recent invention. Discussions about iPads refer to the device as a recent addition to the digital market. Over the first 80 days of its release the iPad sold 3 million devices and that was just over a decade ago. The world of digital appliances is, in comparison to other technical devices, a relatively new 'kid on the block.' It has become clear that the responsibility lies with parents to take cognizance of the harm too much screen time can have on children.

Co-viewing at a young age is recommended so a parent can tune into what is being watched and interact with the child. When the parent is satisfied their child is interacting with the program and not just staring blankly at the screen then it is suggested that would be the time to leave the child to view unsupervised for a short time. The overall opinion is that children under the age of three do not really gain intellectual development from watching a screen. They learn language and interaction with others through communication on a one-to-one basis or within the family group. There is no substitute for this real-life learning.

The overall consensus of opinion is a great deal depends on how children are using screen time and media and what are they watching. Parents need to step in here and monitor the screen time and the caliber of programs being watched. Keeping open immunization with your child about what they are watching helps to protect children from watching undesirable programs

Are there positives to watching screens and being involved in digital devices? This is the other side of the coin the face of the opposite side of the argument. In a debate there would be two sides putting forward their argument. If you were on the pro side of screen time what would you have to say?

The first reaction to the screen your child is watching is the sigh of relief when your child is engaged in something and you breathe for a moment. Using a digital device as an ongoing babysitter is probably the worst habit that has come out of examining screen time but let's look at the good that could be part of this baby-sitting system if it were monitored responsibly with boundaries in mind.

What are the positives of giving children screen time?

- There is a definite correlation between educational programs and learning from screen time. School related programs may reinforce schoolwork and broaden children's general knowledge. During difficult times when children were unable to attend their schools digital screens became the blackboards and tutors for the children who were fortunate to have access to online teaching.

- Video games and digital apps can improve eye hand coordination. Children do enjoy playing digital games and in moderation they do have their place.
- Older children, who can communicate through mobile phones with family and friends, are at an advantage should the need arise to contact someone. This is a great safety device and helpful when school arrangements or parents' plans may change.
- Learning songs, colors and shapes and counting activities are made colorful and entertaining through screen time for younger viewers. Having an adult involved just adds more value to the activity for very young children where supervision and social interaction is important.
- Storytelling, of good value children's stories, can be brought to life for children. However, the real benefit lies in quality of language. Parents should check the quality of the language and the suitability for younger viewers.

The pros and cons of screen time clearly come down to parental management. Undoubtedly screen time has become part of everyday life in the last decade and therefore responsible parents are wanting guidelines to follow when it comes to managing screen time at home.

Parents will need to know what it is their children are watching and some guidelines to appropriate watching would be helpful. Look at these suggestions for responsible screen time.

1. Set limits to the amount of screen time you allow to each child depending on their age group. Be consistent with the time allocations and enforce the regulations, perhaps exceptions are made over the weekend or during the holidays, but the time limit is the time limit.
2. Have zones in your house that are screen free zones. Enforce the rules for example no screen time during mealtimes. No screen time in the bedroom at bedtimes. No smart phone use while driving – be an example to your children. Find other family orientated areas where you would prefer to have no screen time.
3. Emphasize the value of the devices used for educational purposes. Help your child to see the value of learning about their environment or the world around them through this connection with the internet. Show children how they can research so many new things. How they can learn crafts and try science experiments to develop their interest in different hobbies.
4. Be conscious of parental control over what the children watch or learn about. Set limits on their accessibility to programs that would not be suitable for their age group.
5. Be a good role model. Your child is watching and taking their lead from you. If you are constantly on your smart phone or computer when you could be spending quality time with your child, you are not being a good role model. Be sure to practice what you preach, and your children will follow your lead.
6. Provide other activities so your child has opportunities to be

part of everyday normal experiences and practical things to do. Take a walk in the park or visit a friend and make cookies in the kitchen while you sing nursery rhymes together. Screen time cannot provide those kinds of wonderful parent and child bonding activities.

CHILD DEVELOPMENT OPPORTUNITIES FROM POSITIVE DISCIPLINE

Positive discipline or PD is a parenting style that is focused on the idea that children are not inherently bad, but there are behaviors children manifest that are not condoned and considered bad behavior. Positive discipline takes those behaviors, and through positive interaction with children, turns misbehavior into learning opportunities for children.

HERE ARE FIVE CONCEPTS BEHIND POSITIVE DISCIPLINE TO BE ABLE TO USE THIS MODEL OF PARENTING.

1. Communication needs to be effective to benefit from this model of parenting.
2. Discipline is considered a teaching tool and guides children.

It is not permissive, but has guidelines that teach children through their mistakes.
3. Positive discipline is focused on finding solutions to problems not punishment.
4. The center of this model of discipline is mutual respect. Parents and children build respect for one another.
5. Parents try to resolve issues by understanding the root cause behind the problem.

These basic concepts give a good foundation to the principles behind positive parenting and will help parents with how they manage their children's behavior. The positive parenting model aims to always find positive outcomes.

Instead of seeing every incident of misbehavior as an element of bad behavior, positive discipline sees these events as opportunities for learning and growing. 'Time out,' a common form of discipline, becomes 'time in.' The children learn through spending time in with their parents. It is an opportunity to grow in character and understanding of how to behave.

Does positive discipline work with very young children? Yes, it does work but the level of expectation is different as children are still learning to communicate and build a trusting bond with their parents. Here are a few simple ideas of how to direct positive discipline at a young age.

Redirection is a positive discipline tactic.

Positive discipline redirects children to take part in another activity if they are having difficulty dealing with their present moment.

Practice 'time in' and not 'time out.'

Using time in gives parents a chance to speak, one-on-one with their child, to get to the underlying cause of the action. It is a time to try and let the child get in touch with their emotions to understand why they may have felt anger, disappointment or frustration.

Give short and simple reminders.

Using short reminders or cue words to help children understand what is required of them rather than shouting long tirades of directions.

Use positive affirmation.

Finding times to praise children for the good they are doing or the obstacles they have overcome is a very important part of positive parenting. In this way children see the positive things they can do.

Understanding this method of discipline, and putting it into practice, may seem complicated. However, it is not at all difficult once you understand the principles and characteristics behind positive discipline.

Here are some of the underlying principles of positive discipline. The idea behind knowing these principles is to help to make positive discipline a part of your family life.

PRINCIPLE # 1

This form of parenting is focused on trust, kindness, and connection with your child. It changes the way you respond to bad behavior. Your response to discipline is more understanding and supportive. Although you are kind you are also firm and set boundaries you adhere to. Your child knows when they have stepped over a boundary and you help them work through this. A thorough understanding of the stage of development they are at is important. You also need to know of their level of understanding of the offensive action. This is the teaching part of positive parenting as you can explain why your child's action caused hurt or pain to someone else.

PRINCIPLE # 2

Children should feel safe and protected during the times they are being disciplined. Parents are teaching and guiding during this time as they show their children right and wrong. Positive discipline is veering away from verbal and physical punishment that causes fear, distrust, and loss of self-esteem. Positive discipline helps children feel motivated to follow their parents lead and develop good character.

PRINCIPLE # 3

Mastering the positive parenting role model may take some adjustment because it is probably different to the parenting style you were raised with, but once you are familiar with the principles and start to see the results, you will be encouraged to follow the positive parenting way.

Here are some suggestions of how you can incorporate positive parenting into the way you raise your children using these ideas in a more positive and encouraging way.

Keep your calm mantra

Try to address the problem calmly and avoid long lectures dragging out a punishment. Keep the disciplinary talk short and sweet.

Be consistent

Have your guidelines to what your boundaries are and hold fast to those limits. Be firm but fair.

Try to be a good role model

Incorporate mindfulness and empathy into your approach to parenting. Your children will see the difference and respect you for your different attitude towards them and how they behave.

Take action as soon as possible

Try to deal with the problem as quickly and as easily as possible. Be realistic at the time and take into account the underlying root of the problem. Is your child tired, hungry, ready to go home? Consider the circumstances you are in.

Give positive affirmation

Tell your child the good you see in them often.

One of the key factors in this powerful tool of positive parenting is the parent. Parenting can be really tough sometimes and often knowing what to do is not the same as how to get it done. Having some ideas of how to become a positive parent should help parents with this style of parenting. Just a few ideas of how to become a part of this positive parenting ideology.

1. Use your calm voice

Take a deep breath and speak calmly and slowly if you find yourself in a situation where all you want to do is yell. Shouting does not achieve anything. It builds barriers between parents and children.

2. Make physical connections

Give out hugs or make physical connections whenever you can. Snuggle up and read a book. Making time for some physical touch will always bring you closer physically and mentally to your child.

3. Let yourself be reassured

Tell yourself you are doing your best. Everything about being a parent takes some readjusting and you are doing your best.

4. Link in with your child through eye contact

When you are spending time with your child make a conscious effort to hold their attention through making clear eye contact and showing your child you are really listening to them.

5. Leave some time open

Leave some time in your day to sit and play together. Put calls on hold and pencil in playtime to your diary. Playing with your child will help the social aspect of positive parenting and help you connect.

6. Show ways to be kind

Let your child see ways in which you show kindness to others and to them. They will want to copy you and showing kindness is a key part of positive discipline.

7. Attract attention to the positive

Start noticing little things that are positive in your child. Look out for little ways your child is showing their good side.

8. Try to be real

Show your children who you are not who you are pretending to be or think you ought to be. Show your feelings. Apologize if you are wrong and let them know you are not perfect, but you are trying to do your best.

9. Keep your goals in mind

Remember you have goals for your family and positive parenting is one of the ways you are going to reach those goals. When you keep your eye on the goal then the parenting skills you implement have a greater purpose.

10. Decide to be a positive parent

Don't be put off by all the references to an authoritarian style of discipline. Make sure you have the principles of positive parenting in your mind and start to act on them. You may make mistakes as you go along but that doesn't mean you have not tried to be positive in your parenting and in your discipline.

One of the key principles behind positive parenting is using opportunities needing some form of discipline to become learning curves and times for individual growth. How can this be done when you are probably feeling impatient and would normally have reacted differently.

What can you do to make every situation an opportunity for growth? It is not easy just to have a change of heart. You might be following the old school type of parenting and now you have an idea there is something better out there. You want to be a part of this new approach, but you are still a little skeptical. Positive parenting is a way of responding to your child's emotional needs in a sensitive way. Positive parenting keeps development stages in mind as well as feelings and emotional development.

WHAT SHOULD A PARENT DO WHEN A SITUATION ARISES?

- Ask yourself does your child need some help with something. How can you, the parent help with a basic need at that time. Tune into the child's needs and emotions with sensitivity rather than immediately thinking of a punishment to give out and get them to do what you want without any sensitivity.

- Think in terms of problem solving and not trying to control a behavior you deem unacceptable. Think beyond the behavior. Yes, you don't like the way your child is behaving, but with some relevant problem-solving skills you may be able to turn the situation around. When you offer a solution to the problem you show your child, they could have done the same and saved a great deal of anxiety.
- Be respectful of both your needs. You are both family members in this crisis. Respect your child's feelings and manage respect for your own too. Teach your child about respect through a behavioral incident where respect was lacking.
- Recognize the developmental stages your child is going through. Ask yourself do they have the reasoning power to solve this situation or are they ready for this stage of physical development. Acknowledging their developmental levels will make some of your parenting decisions a whole lot easier. You will find it is possible to take on the role of teacher where a child is not ready for a relevant behavior. Rather be the teacher than law enforcement.
- Avoid punishments like spanking, time-out, name calling, and shaming your child. As you read these forms of punishment and learn about positive discipline, they may make you feel very uncomfortable. That is a good thing. It

shows you recognize how far from positive parenting, and positive discipline, these forms of punishment are.

There will always be skeptics and naysayers as you try to do your best to be a positive parent. Recognize there are some enemies out there ready to squash your best efforts.

WHAT ARE SOME OF THE ENEMIES OF POSITIVE DISCIPLINE?

#1.

You may be surprised to read that you are your own worst enemy and you could be the one who sabotages your efforts to become a member of the Positive Parenting Club! This is because you are often the one who says the most negative things about yourself. You need to stop talking negatively to yourself as this breaks down your confidence as a parent.

#2.

Questioning if you are doing everything just right. The perfect parent is a fairy tale, a fantasy. Trying to be perfect is going to frustrate you and your children. Your mindset should rather be to try and DO your best and not have to BE the best. Look at choosing the right path for your family and trying to guide everyone along that path. That is more attainable and won't leave you feeling defeated.

#3.

Wondering if we are good enough. Any parent thinks from time to time that they are not good enough for the role of parent. Thinking like that too often sews self-doubt and this kind of negative talk makes it more difficult to try new skills because wondering about our abilities as a parent makes it more difficult to be a parent.

#4.

We make unfair comparisons. We live in a very competitive world and may be tempted to make unrealistic comparisons between ourselves and other parents and their children. Social media can erode our confidence in ourselves and our children because of the opportunity to make comparisons. These comparisons lead to discontent and doubt about your own parenting skills which may be perfectly fine and suit your family very well.

#5.

Too much stress in your life. Parenting is not for the faint hearted and can be exhausting. Parents are always better at being parents when they are relaxed and not overly stressed. If being overly stressed is affecting your parenting style, then try to find ways to get some stress relief. Get children involved around the house. Make time for yourself by sharing the parenting load. Managing your time is an important factor too. Make sure you have a schedule that allows you some 'off time.'

#6.

Don't get caught in comparisons. Every parent, child and family are unique, and your parenting skills may be under scrutiny. Stand firm and don't let comparisons pull you down.

When you feel you are facing a negative comment, or your parenting seems to be on shaky ground try to turn your thoughts around at that precise moment. Look for the way to use the incident as a teaching opportunity. Allow mistakes to happen and remember:

"Discipline is helping a child solve a problem. Punishment is making a child suffer for having a problem. To raise problem solvers, focus on solutions, not retributions."

— L.R. KNOST - AUTHOR OF 'TWO THOUSAND KISSES A DAY.'

13

SPEAKING AND LISTENING SKILLS

As an adult and a parent, you expect your children to listen to you. Unfortunately, that is not always the case. Speaking and listening are skills. Parents as well as children need to learn how to do both of these means of communication. Parenting and positive discipline are very difficult without being able to speak to your child and have them listen in return.

Here is the - * HOW, * WHAT, * WHY, * WHERE AND *WHEN of talking to children.

Guidelines of different opportunities to talk to children and find they are listening to you.

THE HOW:

- Getting your child's attention and focus on you is the most important how of connection with your child.
- It means going down to their level to make eye contact so your child can focus on you specifically.
- Say their name when you talk to them. This gets their attention, and they engage with you as you say their name, make contact, and then your request.
- Make your interaction on a personal basis. Don't yell from the other side of the house or garden. Go to where your child is and speak about what you want them to do. In this way they will prioritize what you are asking.
- Speak on the correct language level. The younger the child the shorter the sentences and the less instructions the better.
- Give your child a choice sometimes. Just a quick choice between two things. 'Do you want cereal or toast?' for example. Simple choices of things around the home.

THE WHAT:

- What you say is important. Aim to be positive and use the word 'no' less if you can. Instead of no jumping on the couch say...child's name, we sit on the couch.
- Give fair warning of leaving for an event. Your child needs time to get ready. They will feel better about having to go if they know it is happening soon.

SPEAKING AND LISTENING SKILLS | 367

- Try 'what did I say?' and ask your child to repeat what you said to see if they have listened. Keep the instruction short so you know they can repeat it to you.
- Say what you want by starting with 'I want you to...' In that way your child knows what it is they need to do.
- Say what you mean in a way they will understand. Try not to ask 'why' rather say let's talk about what you did when…. Children often can't answer why, and the problem may be better understood if you as to talk about what they did.

THE WHY:

- Think about why you are making your request to your child and this will help you phrase it correctly and in the right tone of voice.
- Why you ask something of a child is a good time to get in touch with their feelings or convey yours. You can say how you feel when they are not listening.

THE WHEN:

- Timing is important with trying to get a child to listen. When children have other needs like sleep, a meal or just to go home it is difficult to talk sensibly to them.
- When children are clearly upset by something it will not be a great time to talk to them. Make a clear short request and try

to settle their emotional upset before trying to start with your positive discipline approach.
- Use the tactic of 'when and then.' This works very well to try and teach consequences. When whatever you want done is done then there will be something done for your child.

THE WHERE:

- Ideally your conversation should take place in the space where you needed to say something. Go to where you want something done.
- Explain safety rules in the place where the safety awareness is relevant if at all possible. Use books to explain relevant information as a talking tool.
- Learn about table manners and behavior at mealtimes by having meals together.

Keeping an eye on the how, what, why, when, and where will make a difference to the talking times you have with our child. It will just make you think conscientiously of the way you talk to your child.

Talking to your child should begin from infancy. Here is how the knowledge of developmental phases and the skill of talking to a child go hand in hand. The growth for children in this area is rapid, and huge steps are taken. Knowing what to expect and what input to be prepared for adds to the development of communication between you and your child.

Development of communication from babies through the toddler stage and more:

Birth and infancy.

Building communication skills starts from birth with gentle interaction and loving touch as the infant feels safe and loved during this time the baby and infant are listening to sounds, watching facial expressions and recognizing body language. When your baby makes babbling noises babble back as a way to engage in this early stage of conversation.

Talking to toddlers.

Toddlers are learning words at a rapid rate. They are starting to make little three- or four-word phrases and begin to understand requests from their parents. They don't have the vocabulary to express big ideas or events, but they are learning about communication all the time. When you are with your toddler give them the words to describe what you are doing, let them repeat after you anything you are dong together. Correct them calmly by repeating what they have said in a kind manner to help them with their conversation. Give toddlers time to find the right words and then help them with learning a new word. Watch their body language and ways of communicating through pointing at objects. Give them the words they are looking for.

Learning songs and rhymes is a great way to teach toddlers language. If your toddler is at a preschool find out what songs they are learning and you can sing them at home together. While you are playing, tell your toddler what you are doing and in this way, they learn the words for the action they are experiencing. The more you play together and say words for the actions the more your child is going to learn to speak the language you are introducing at home.

Talking to preschoolers.

Now your child has moved up the communication scale. These little people are starting to use language to describe their world and their feelings. They are using longer sentences and beginning to describe their feelings. Preschoolers learn by asking loads of questions. They want to know about the world around them. Their span of attention has increased, and they are able to tell stories and hold conversations. Show your child you are listening to them and give them your full attention when you can. Your preschooler has a lot of words now and can string them together if their stories are getting too long and you have something else to do suggest they finish at that moment quickly or save the rest of the story for later.

You will hear many 'why' questions. Try to answer them fairly. Take the answering of questions seriously and try to find the right answer. If you don't know tell your preschooler, you will look for the answer. You can do that together if your child is interested. Reading and looking at books with your child helps to broaden their outlook and increase their vocabulary.

Early Primary school years.

This is an exciting stage when words and sounds come together, and children start to read for themselves and write as well as spell. Children are able to hold more adult conversations. If you suspect any significant language delays or speech problems, it is important to get that sorted sooner rather than later. Your child's teacher will be able to give you input too if your child is not coping at school.

There are two sides to our communication abilities. Talking and listening, and listening is a skill. How do we learn to listen? Is it a natural process or does it have to be taught? Basically, when parents want their children to listen, they want to know if their child can hear their voice. Parents want to know if their child can fade out background noises and tune into their parents' voice. Do children have the ability to understand the meaning behind the sentences and can they interpret their meaning fully?

Actually, it is no surprise that some children do struggle to listen. This skill is subject to their stage of development, their cognitive ability, and their health at the time of receiving the message. A listening skill needs practice and encouragement. Following the developmental steps will help parents to understand what the skills are and to help with their development.

Listening actually requires three processes. Hearing, listening, and paying attention.

1. Hearing

The infant's hearing begins to develop in the womb. At this very early stage the baby develops the ability to hear. Soon after being born the baby will react to the mother's voice. Some children may be born with a hearing impairment or disability. Sometimes they suffer hearing loss because of infections.

2. Listening

Babies start listening and turning their heads towards a sound from about four months of age. As they grow, they start to hear the difference between sounds around them and in particular their mother's voice. As they develop and grow, they are able to identify sounds and recognize them in words and sentences. These skills help children with phonetic understanding and lead to being able to read. While they can listen to sounds, they need to be able to pay attention at the same time to focus on listening for longer periods of time.

3. Paying attention

The third component is paying attention. Children go through five stages of paying attention.

1. The distractable phase from 0 – 1 year. Early attempts at holding their attention are not easily made at this age.
2. The single channel attention span from 1 – 2 years. During this phase the child can focus on one thing at a time. They do not like to be distracted from this at all.
3. The more flexible single channel phase from 2 – 3 years. This is where they can begin to shift from one activity to another.
4. The double channel attention at about 4 to 5 years and they can focus their attention from an activity to a speaker.
5. Fully integrated attention comes from 5 years onward. Child should be able to focus their attention on various sizes of groups and ignore some distractions. They can hold their attention for a longer length of time.

It is important to note not all children will reach these goals at the same time. This is a guideline only.

Children with poor listening skills will struggle to pay attention and poor listening skills will impact on their schoolwork. Listening enables children to develop their vocabulary, improve their language skills, and their comprehension. When children reach their primary school phase and are learning to read and write and spell, they will need to be able to listen and process sounds through auditory processing.

Listening with comprehension is another important part of listening skills. This form of listening enables your child to understand the meaning of words and relate to them. Listening comprehension allows a child to listen to a story, understand what it is about and talk about the story. They may even be able to remember it and retell the story to someone else. These are all skill building effects from listening comprehension. Good listeners become good at communicating with others.

Here are some suggestions of ways to improve listening skills when your child is ready for this.

- Make a conscious effort to plan some kind of listening activity into your day. It could be a game, listening to a story, having fun with musical games like musical statues or singing rhymes and songs together.
- Help your child build up their vocabulary. Books with pictures and words or simple stories are vocabulary builders during the early stages of acquiring words. Flash cards,

games, and children's programs geared specifically for building vocabulary help enormously.
- Keep your activities short and sweet because most young children have a short span of attention.

How do you discipline a child who won't listen?

This can be one of the most frustrating aspects of parenting. You want to teach your child, but they repeatedly defy you and do not want to listen. This makes a parent feel they have no control over their child and no influence in disciplining them.

One of the reasons for deliberately not listening is attributed to a power struggle going on. Although you may not be fully aware of it your child can use ignoring you as a way to have some power over you through deliberately not listening to you. If your child can hear and listen most of the time when they want to then not listening to you in particular could be part of a power struggle mentality. When children choose not to listen, they are taking control of the situation. They are using their bodies and their attitude to have power in the relationship. This could be an opportunity for you as the parent to let go of some of the control you have and let your child make some choices. Not major choices, but some little ones like what to wear and the story they may choose. Involve them in some of the household chores and just try to relinquish some of the power you have without realizing you have taken complete control.

Think about offering your child a choice. Giving them an either/or choice in decision making relinquishes some power their way and helps with decision making skills. When there is no choice the request comes across as an order and perhaps your child would listen more carefully if the request came with a choice. Then your child has to think about the choices and make a decision.

Be consistent in your requests. Being consistent allows your child to feel comfortable in your expectations. You could have a countdown to get the job done. This helps your child know that within the countdown space they have certain things to do and that is the stable expectancy they need.

Model good communication skills yourself and help to show your child you are a good listener, and you do what is expected of you around the house. You are prepared to help out with tidying up, but you are not prepared to accept a messy room and your child is called to answer for their room too.

Although you may be feeling very frustrated during one of your child's bouts of not listening try your level best not to yell. Yelling and screaming at children achieves nothing. Children will turn off their listening button in the face of yelling and your words and high volume of energy will be wasted.

Yelling does not work. It causes fear and negativity. Yelling takes away from any learning opportunities associated with helping and listening. Yelling simply makes your child feel they have to comply and that there is no way they can be an integral part of the action. They just feel pushed into following orders.

What can you do instead? Here are some suggestions.

- Don't just say no all the time while you yell at your child and what they are doing. Turn the conversation around and have a positive slant by asking your child to do something positive. Instead of yelling no running as you all get out of the car turn the conversation to now, we are all going to walk or let's walk to the house. If the request is ignored, then some time in would be warranted to explain why walking inside is the best option.
- Take time for a pause and a deep breath before continuing with your instructions. Offer to help with the chore and show that working together is a good way to get things done.

14

HOW TO GO FROM BATTLEFIELD TO PEACEFUL PLACE

Clearly every family would like their home to be a haven.

Just like Dorothy from the Wizard of Oz who says:

"There is no place like home."

And then with a click of her ruby slippers, Dorothy, played by Judy Garland in the 1939 musical, gets right back to her home in Kansas.

Those slippers have become one of the most valuable items of film memorabilia and would certainly buy Dorothy a grand home, far removed from the humble shack she lived in, when the tornado struck. Does your home feel like it has been hit by a tornado sometimes? Or do you think it is actually a war zone, a battlefield?

> "The battlefield is a scene of chaos. The winner will be the one who controls that chaos both his own and his enemies."
>
> — NAPOLEON BONAPARTE - A FRENCH MILITARY LEADER DURING THE FRENCH REVOLUTION

Would this quote describe your home? Are you trying to be the one who controls the chaos? Do you worry about how the chaos could be affecting your child? Chaos does affect family life. It is characterized by disorganization and confusion, and it has a negative effect on children. Everyone wants to find a peaceful home. No one wants a battlefield.

Household chaos is a valid term used by researchers into the effects of home life on children. Growing up in a home that is noisy and has no set routine and is a home where children never know what could happen next is detrimental to the environment parents should try to have to raise their children. Household chaos is measured by the level of disorganization and confusion in the home and these elements have an adverse effect on children. Studies into these effects have shown that household chaos impacts on cognitive development, literacy, social, and emotional development. Family, or household chaos, is directly linked to family routines or lack of them and negativity in parents who are affected by this chaos too.

CHAOS is an acronym for:

C - Confusion
H - Hubbub
A - and
O - Order scale

Confusion reflecting the lack of organization and boundaries in the home creating an organized environment for the whole family.

Hubbub is descriptive of the noise levels as everyone is fighting for their voice to be heard above the chaos.

And

Order scale goes back to the lack of order or scale of organization as there is no routine or little structure to the family life.

These home environments are referred to by family and friends with comments like:

> "It's like living in a zoo at our house."

Or

> "When I am at home I can't hear myself think!"

Chaos in the home or the battlefield mentality is linked to disruptive behavior at school where children carry over their lifestyle of coping in unruly environments.

This type of home environment can be changed and introducing the model of positive parenting together with a positive discipline style of control is the way to restore order into your home. It will take a team effort and a conscious decision to change but it can be done.

"When a team takes hold of its problems the problem gets solved. It is true on the battlefield, it is true in business, and it is true in life."

— JOCKO WILLINK

Jocko Willink is an American author and retired navy SEALs officer.

If you are desperately floundering in a sea of chaos at home, then take a naval officer's advice and get your team together to tackle the chaos. The opposite of chaos is order and therefore it makes sense to restore order to your home environment.

Here are some practical tips on how to start.

It will seem overwhelming at first if your home is an OTT (Over the Top) chaotic environment, but start small with baby steps and work your way forward. Tell yourself

"Love begins at home," a short and sweet quote from Mother Teresa.

Whatever you are doing, you are doing out of love for your family.

Step one

Take a few moments to organize your mind and your mental state with regard to the changes you want to make. Write a list and get it all down on paper so you have an orderly idea of what you are going to tackle. This is your battle plan.

Step Two

Do one small thing that will bring you pride and joy. Just clean the sink or tidy a bookcase or sort out your desk. Any small thing done each day will get you to feel less chaotic. Admire your handiwork and check your list. Give yourself a tick. You have made a small advancement on the battlefield.

Step Three

Create a calm and quiet space for yourself. Yes, as the team leader you will need a place that is yours. No toys thrown about, no invasion of other people's property. A safe haven just for you to escape to. If it is your bedroom or your study or any space, however small you can call your own, then go and claim it and make it your own. Put a boundary line in place. Tell the family how they should behave in your special space. This is your 'ops room' where your strategies for solving family issues takes place.

Step Four

Pinpoint three particular areas that are causing your stress levels to skyrocket. Although you might be feeling stress everywhere it is important to take a deep breath and look for the worst spots to do a good positive job to sort them out. Dedicate a problem-solving page for each and systematically decide how to resolve the problem. It could be some form of disorganization in your home, or perhaps it is a behavior you find in your child that is really bothersome. Does this behavior happen at the same time of the day or is it all day? Ask yourself when it is that you are most stressed and then deal with the problem, time, or behavior.

Here is a short description of a way to do this while you are still at the planning stage of your battle plan.

On your planner write:

- What the problem is.....
- What can I do about it...
- Then have some steps in place to solve the problem. Be honest with yourself if you are the problem, then starting from the inside out will help reach the victory point faster. If there is a particularly difficult time of day, perhaps your routine is out of kilter. If it is a particular action from your child, perhaps the root problem is your parenting style, and some positive discipline is in order.

Step Five

Rally the troops. Now you have your battle plan start with your parenting partner and discuss the plans you have for bringing order back into the chaos. Explain your motives and have a second in command on your side. Look at what you can do together. Decide on some family values and be ready to share those with the family. Look at the ages of your children and take into account their developmental levels and their ability to focus on your plans. Getting everyone to buy into the new routines and the plans is very important.

Step Six

Have a family get together where you and your partner explain the new regime. Everyone needs to be onboard. Each member of the family is given a responsibility that is manageable for their age. Everyone is told family mealtime is not negotiable. The whole family will sit together for a meal. Start small and specify how often family mealtimes happen according to the schedule of the family. You could break this news at a family meal when everyone is sitting together, and you have a captive audience.

Step Seven

Create family routines. Set aside three times in the day when you would like there to be some organized routine. Think morning, noon and night for your three key times and start with one of them. Work out the routine and get the family on board to implement it.

You could put up a chart like this one for your family routines. Everyone will be different, so these are just guidelines and always have room for flexibility

MORNING:	NOON:	NIGHT:
Wake up and get dressed.	Arrive home or be at school for after school care and sports	Bath time and getting ready for supper and bedtime.
Have breakfast.	Have lunch snack and some relax time.	Enjoy family meal together.
Brush teeth	Unpack your school bag and do homework.	Brush teeth and get ready for bed.
Comb hair look tidy	Read something from a book or study.	Bedtime story and quiet ending to the day.
Check school bag.	Pack away your homework Have free time or recreational sports.	Say goodnight and lights out sleep tight till the morning.
Get ready for the bus or Mom's taxi.	Tidy your room if necessary.	Time for parents to have their own personal time and space.
Enjoy your morning at school.	Be grateful for an afternoon spent learning and having fun.	Sleep peacefully in a chaos free environment.

Charts like this are just a guide and make everyone feel there is a plan, and the idea is to win the battle over chaos and find order in the home and the routine.

Just simply having a routine will make a huge difference to the inner peace and tranquility of the home. A routine lowers stress levels and provides a foundation of peace and calm for the family to follow. The routine adds more time to the day because the time is structured and even time for freedom of choice is available. Families who follow a routine experience lower stress levels, better health habits and they feel more productive.

Having a routine will definitely help you to get out of the chaos mold and into a healthier lifestyle.

Once you have tackled the chaos that surrounded the family living space and how the family led their lives on a day-to-day basis then turn your focus to the positive parenting skills and implement positive discipline in your home.

How do you begin to implement positive parenting and in particular positive discipline.

> *"Provide plenty of love balanced by structure and discipline."*
>
> — BARACK OBAMA

Here are some suggestions on how to bring in that structure and discipline while starting out with positive parenting. It is these concepts that will support your mission to be a positive parent and bring peace into your home.

Here are 7 tips towards gaining peace in your home through positive parenting.

1. Put reasonable boundaries in place

Boundaries are there to protect you as a parent so you in turn can provide the best parenting skills for your child. Boundaries communicate a respect for parents and teaching children to respect is a good life skill for the present and for the future when they may become parents too.

2. Aim to be firm, but loving at the same time

Treating children with a firm but loving tone of voice helps children to feel secure in your parenting model. Keep your disciplinary tone of voice moderate, not yelling, but firm and consistent.

3. Use natural consequences as a way to teach your child

There are many great opportunities to use natural consequences to enforce a point about following through with the correct behavior. Toddlers in particular are wanting to defy parenting standards. The little voice that says no all the time and refuses to put a jacket on in cold weather could feel the consequence of being cold on an outing. You would of course have packed a jacket in the car but let your toddler feel the cold and the consequence of not taking a jacket so they can realize that mom or dad were right and should be listened to. These are natural consequences that lead to learning lessons.

4. Help children see the logic in your parenting discipline

Helping children to see a logic behind your disciplinary action is another helpful way to start with positive parenting. Keeping puzzles tidy for example means the puzzle can be completed later and none of the pieces will go missing. That means there is logic in packing away carefully.

5. Be a good role model and show respect for one another

If you want your children to have respect for you as a parent, then it is important to show respect to your children. It is a case of follow my lead and show kindness and gentleness with others if that is what you would like to have shown to you. Practice saying please and thank you as a measure of respect. Help children to look at good role models and to be willing to copy their qualities.

6. Develop feelings of Empathy

Know what and how your child can behave at certain stages of their life. This will enable you to relate to the milestones you are going through and help you to empathize. At the same time share empathy with your children.

7. Work on 'time-in' rather than 'time-out.'

Time in is a powerful tool. The time in principle works on the fact that the child is taken away from the situation where they misbehaved and together with their parents receives some time in one-on-one session with one of their parents. During this time parent and child can look at the situation and the child will be disciplined accordingly.

8. Learn how to connect with your children

Communication on the right level is a very important part of positive parenting. This means being able to understand what your child is capable of at their specific milestones and building that connection through play and spending quality time with your child. It is a process of bonding from an early age. When your child is born that bond starts to grow and every bit of time you put into building that relationship will count in building a great relationship with your child.

9. Spend time on family activities

Bonding with the family as a whole creates special memories and a family ethos to share.

10. Have a parenting style of unconditional love

Teach your child through love and positive parenting that however many mistakes they make they are still loved and cherished by you and are a very important part of your household.

"Childhood is fleeting, so let kids be kids and cherish the time you have together." Words of wisdom from Abraham Lincoln. The 16th president of America who knew all about chaos as he led the nation through the American Civil War.

Bringing peace into your home is probably the most sought-after attribute to parenting. It is the desired outcome from all the parenting input through trying to score with positive parenting and your new style of discipline. Think about what peace in the home means to you. Your home may not always look and sound peaceful. Children have energy and are busy but the underlying feeling from your perspective should be one of peace in the home. This feeling comes from putting in place the blocks that build the boundaries surrounding positive parenting. When you have a solid foundation to build on and you can refer to the style of parenting you believe in you should start to feel that peace.

There is a dear little plant called affectionately 'Peace in the home.' This little plant needs some sunshine, not too much, warmth and water. It loves to be in the kitchen the nourishing part of the home.

Peace in the home, if you have it and grow it successfully, will grace your kitchen as an example of peace while it gives off oxygen to help with your clean air. Share peace in your home and watch your children grow.

"When you invite people into your home, you invite them to yourself."

— OPRAH WINFREY

Keep those words in mind and add a peace in your home plant too. Then through a connection with nature and nurturing your children you will be able to face the battles and come out victorious.

CONCLUSION

Now you have read the book, taken note of the parenting tips and hopefully fueled your plane ready to fly with two wings intact and a tank full of unconditional love. This positive parenting book, with the advice on how to discipline with guilt free intentions, has the two wings to your plane. The knowledge and the skill referred to by Wilbur Wright way back in the days when aviation first started.

This book aimed to help you aviate, navigate, and communicate through your parenting journey. There may have been turbulence along the way, but with chapters giving you insight into child development and the early years of a toddler's life, you should have had a better idea of how to put new skills into practice. Taking a good look at different parenting styles through the parenting audit should help you see what to do and what to avoid. The indicators and reminders of good and bad parenting gives parents a chance to assess where their skills lie at this present moment. No one is perfect, but everyone can take steps to improve their skills and knowledge.

Change does not always come easily and finding good role models when you embark on something new is a challenge. Finding out you should be a good role model may not be easy either. It has been said that children remember far more of how their parents made them feel that what they had them do. Getting in touch with your feelings, as well as your child's feelings, requires a deep sense of empathy and respect for one another.

This is a practical book, and each chapter has suggestions of how to begin practicing positive parenting. Look at the comparative charts for a well-rounded idea of the to do's and not to do's. Take an honest look in the mirror that describes good and bad parenting. If you recognize any of the qualities mentioned, then take the time to be honest with yourself, and change.

The Serenity Prayer known to many for helping to make changes and be real about what you can and can't change may help in your parenting role.

> It calls for **serenity** to accept the things you cannot change.
> For **courage** to change the things you can,
> And for **wisdom** to know the difference.

Serenity brings peace and calmness to your parenting. Courage is the strength you need to face some of the stressful times. Courage helps you make the changes and face the fear of failure you may have as you step into this new role in your life. Wisdom is the knowledge and experience you will acquire through reading this book. A book you can happily refer to on numerous occasions to boost your morale and to tick the parenting boxes that apply to you personally.

This book may help you to see the difference between what can be changed and what you have to work around in the best possible way. Are you ready to practice unconditional love and learn how to speak and listen to your child? Can you make changes to your idea of screen time based on the advice given in this book? Will you find working on building trust with your child is the answer to so many other problems?

The final chapter in the book speaks of turning your 'Battlefield' into a 'Peaceful Place.' That would be the ultimate recommendation for the book and its contents. Start by resolving the negative problems and chaos in your home and turn the war zone into a place of peace. Use the two wings of the plane, the yin and yang of harmony to improve your environment. See and hear the difference as you build deeper trust and emotional bonds with your children.

There will always be skeptics along the way. The optimists and the pessimists who comment on your journey. There are always two sides to a story and the one can resonate with the other if you look for the positive with the negative.

> *"Both optimists and pessimists contribute to our society,"*

said Gil Stein, an archaeologist, who wrote 'Rethinking World Systems.'

> "The optimist invented the airplane and the pessimist the parachute!"
>
> — GIL STEIN

It is hoped, with all sincerity, that this book will fly your parenting plane sky high with optimism! That you will always have a parachute to rely on when times are tough, and you need a gentle ride down to a happy landing.

THE END.

www.ingramcontent.com/pod-product-compliance
Lightning Source LLC
Chambersburg PA
CBHW030901080526
44589CB00010B/96